"This book is an empowering and insightful read. It is a must-read for women of color seeking to thrive in leadership. Blending timeless biblical principles, decades of executive coaching wisdom, real-world case studies, and actionable advice, it offers a powerful road map for navigating the challenges and opportunities of leadership with grace and impact."
Jessica Shepherd, CEO of Sanctum Med + Wellness and author of *Generation M*

"What if you could sit on the front porch with Lady Wisdom herself, laugh and cry and learn facts that will shift your thinking and lift you up out of your chair? That is what this book is. I am honored to be a friend."
Laurie Beth Jones, author of *Jesus, CEO*; *The Path*; and *Jesus, Life Coach*

"Froswa' Booker-Drew creates a welcoming and informative narrative that embraces the realities of being a Christian woman of color in the workplace. This book provides me, a white female leader, even more insights into the systemic barriers to success that are created in my institution that, quite honestly, are often invisible to me. I value reading the real-life testimonies by Froswa' and others who share their vulnerable experiences here, giving me more fuel to address those challenges within the workplace I run. A must-read for all of us striving to make the world a better place."
Jennifer Bartkowski, CEO of Girl Scouts of Northeast Texas

"In *Front Porch Wisdom*, Froswa' Booker-Drew uses her own rich experience and the lived experiences of women of color to create a playbook for BIPOC women to lead, thrive, and succeed by leaning into their expertise, wisdom, and faith. Froswa' challenges each of us to be hard on institutions, soft on people, and kind to ourselves. By challenging White supremacy culture generally, specifically naming its impact on BIPOC women, Froswa' has created a compelling resource for women of color to use in succeeding professionally and personally because of—not in spite of—their identities, experiences, knowledge, and faith."
Aimee Cunningham, president and CEO of The Boone Family Foundation

"Froswa' Booker-Drew is a rare voice of wisdom and authenticity in the leadership space. *Front Porch Wisdom* is a timely gift, offering the guidance leaders have long needed. Froswa's unique ability to weave biblical principles with practical strategies makes this book a transformative resource for those seeking to lead with faith and purpose."
Lorenzo A. Watson, CEO and president of the Christian Community Development Association

"This book is essential for women of color leaders. Froswa' Booker-Drew provides practical, strategic toolkits—ranging from reflective insights to powerful prayers—designed to create lasting, actionable social impact in our communities. It emphasizes that no matter our background, we all have the ability to lead and make meaningful change."

Jin-Ya Huang, founder of Break Bread, Break Borders

"Froswa' Booker-Drew is a seasoned professional whose extensive experience and profound expertise shine through in *Front Porch Wisdom*. This book is exactly what I wish I had years ago stepping into leadership. It offers timeless insights that continue to resonate with me, and I find myself uncovering new layers of wisdom that will guide and sustain me in my work for years to come."

Bethany Rivera Molinar, executive director of Ciudad Nueva Community Outreach and board chair of the Christian Community Development Association

Foreword by Natasha Sistrunk Robinson

Froswa' Booker-Drew

FRONT PORCH WISDOM

Navigating Leadership Pressures and Barriers as a Woman of Color

An imprint of InterVarsity Press
Downers Grove, Illinois

InterVarsity Press
P.O. Box 1400 | Downers Grove, IL 60515-1426
ivpress.com | email@ivpress.com

©2025 by Soulstice Consultancy, LLC

All rights reserved. No part of this book may be reproduced in any form without written permission from InterVarsity Press.

InterVarsity Press® is the publishing division of InterVarsity Christian Fellowship/USA®. For more information, visit intervarsity.org.

Scripture quotations, unless otherwise noted, have been taken from the World English Bible, which is in the public domain.

While any stories in this book are true, some names and identifying information may have been changed to protect the privacy of individuals.

The publisher cannot verify the accuracy or functionality of website URLs used in this book beyond the date of publication.

Cover design: Faceout Studio, Jeff Miller
Interior design: Jeanna Wiggins
Images: © ibnjaafar / E+ via Getty Images, © CSA Images via Getty Images, © laurien / DigitalVision
 Vectors via Getty Images

ISBN 978-1-5140-0888-1 (print) | ISBN 978-1-5140-0889-8 (digital)

Printed in the United States of America ∞

Library of Congress Cataloging-in-Publication Data
A catalog record for this book is available from the Library of Congress.

32 31 30 29 28 27 26 25 | 12 11 10 9 8 7 6 5 4 3 2 1

This book is dedicated to the women I've worked with over the years who have come to me for wisdom and direction. I didn't start out attempting to be wise. I prayed for it daily and, for some reason, people began asking me to share. I am grateful that you not only sought me out for guidance but that you took my words and lessons to heart. I hope that this book continues to build on the many conversations we've had that were designed to challenge, encourage, and support you. May you feel my love and constant cheering for you to fulfill the destiny God has for you.

To a young woman who is not just a colleague or coworker but who also happens to be my daughter: I know you see your mother in ways others do not. You have witnessed my life in contexts others have not experienced. You don't see me just as your mother but, now that you are an adult, as a woman who is trying to get it right even when I don't always have the answers.

Thank you for loving me and knowing that all I do is in hope that it will be a springboard for you to soar higher and further. I'm so proud of you and I hope you can see a reflection of yourself in the pages of this book. We may resemble one another tremendously in our appearance, but I hope you can also see yourself in the many things I've learned from you shining through my words and my life!

I love you, Kazai Kiara!

Contents

Foreword by Natasha Sistrunk Robinson — 1

Introduction: Sit with Me on the Porch — 5

1. What Do Leadership, Women, and Work Have to Do with It? — 11
2. What Does the Data Say? — 19
3. You Are Not an Impostor — 29
4. Who You Need in Life — 44
5. Rejection and Trauma in the Workplace — 57
6. Intersectionality and Leadership — 72
7. Networking and Social Capital — 80
8. Emotional and Spiritual Intelligence as a Strategy — 92
9. Discrimination in the Workplace — 106
10. The Postracial Society Is an Ideal — 117
11. Interviewing, Negotiating, and Getting the Role — 128
12. The Impact of White Supremacy on Organizational Culture — 139
13. The Case for Diversity, Equity, Inclusion, and Belonging — 152
14. Coaching Up, Power Dynamics, and Change Management — 161

Epilogue: Time to Go Inside from the Porch — 173

Acknowledgments — 175

Appendix: Resources for Connection — 179

Further Reading — 183

Notes — 187

Foreword

NATASHA SISTRUNK ROBINSON

WHEN I FIRST MET DR. FROSWA' BOOKER-DREW, I immediately understood that she was a connector, a well-resourced champion of women of color, and a leadership consultant with invaluable expertise, both formally learned and life tested. We connected right away. Given our mutual passions and areas of expertise, I welcomed the opportunity to become one of her first readers and accepted the publisher's invitation to write the foreword for this book.

You see, I too, am a Black, Christian woman and a leader's leader. Dr. Froswa' and I have both had varied experiences of leading in the marketplace and doing important diversity and equity work before it was popular, and then unpopular. We do this work because of our faith, commitment to justice, and to honor the *imago Dei* in all humans. As an entrepreneur—both a small business owner and nonprofit leader—who reads, consults, coaches, and mentors others, I am always looking for resources to share with my diverse clients and mentees. And I specifically seek out leadership resources that are not authored by White men and women because they do not face the same challenges in the workplace or in ministry that women of color do.

So I am thrilled that Dr. Froswa's *Front Porch Wisdom* is being added to the growing canon of leadership books written by women of color.

In *Front Porch Wisdom*, Dr. Froswa' speaks as a leadership expert, mentor, and coach to all women of color and as an auntie to the next generation of leaders. This is a FUBU offering, a book that is For Us and By Us. Dr. Froswa' understands that Black and Brown people have historically shown our strength and resilience by working and standing together as a collective, so she writes and speaks from that place of unity and communal uplift.

With this collection of shared wisdom, Dr. Froswa' reflects on her own leadership experiences while offering an intergenerational perspective for listening and learning. She is not afraid to address taboo topics that place women of color in the crosshairs of racism and sexism. She is not afraid to name or say the hard-yet-important things to women of color readers about the systems or workplaces we inhabit and the types of people we must navigate along our leadership and professional journeys. I was intrigued by how the disparities shared in some of the case studies—along with the pressure to work twice as hard to get half as much—drove some women of color out of the workplace and into entrepreneurship. Entrepreneurship is not for the faint of heart, and it is not for everyone. However, I hope these stories inspire some readers to take more calculated risks or explore opportunities for multiple streams of income.

It is my desire that this book be read broadly, for throughout it Dr. Froswa' provides cultural context and real-life case studies that are informative for readers who are outside the people group to which she is speaking. Too often, we lack empathy for people's experiences when we have not gone through the same thing, but the book's case studies provide an invitation for personal introspection and corporate training to expose our blind spots, explore our preferences and implicit biases, and give us confidence to confront and speak out against microaggressions and address offenses when they do take place. The cultural context and case studies are important educational tools for those who hire, supervise, and work with women of color, and they are necessary considerations for all who seek to call themselves an ally, mentor, sponsor, or supporter of women of color.

Writing as a Christian woman means that Dr. Froswa' has included Scripture throughout the book to inspire and center her reader, and the questions offered can be used both as a coaching tool and as spiritual practices for journaling, reflection, or group discussion. However, there is something else that I hope the diverse readership takes away from this book. I recall former First Lady Michelle Obama sharing her frustration for how often she observes men being given the opportunity to fail up within the workspace.[1] In other words, some men (especially White men) can be given a leadership opportunity, completely blow it, and then keep their jobs without additional scrutiny. Or they can receive a lateral transfer or promotion within the company or even get hired for a better position at another company. Many women, especially women of color, are not extended the same opportunities, especially if they lack the social or relational capital to cushion their fall. So in addition to the wisdom shared throughout the book, one thing I want all readers to pay attention to concerning the pressures and barriers of leadership is the lack of grace that is extended to women of color who lead within the workplace.

As a leader who does purposeful and intentional work that affects people's lives, shifts culture, and changes systems, I believe it is important that we cultivate communities of competent leaders of character. I also believe that it takes courage to cultivate leaders who will challenge themselves and grow their skills and capacity, leaders who do not internalize or personalize their failures or have their failures remain as a scarlet letter, but instead use their failures as feedback and opportunities for growth. This type of care is what separates humans from robots and values the person beyond their productivity.

I believe in you, women of color. I believe that you were born to lead. I believe that God predestined your purpose and path for leadership before the foundations of the earth. I believe that once you get clarity about that purpose and path, you can courageously join God in the redemptive work that is happening in every sphere of influence in this earth. We need the light of your leadership to shine brightly for his glory. And when you get tired or weary on the journey, just come back to the front porch to rest a little while and gain more wisdom over some tea or coffee. There are many of us who are ready and willing to offer support as you navigate the way ahead.

Introduction

Sit with Me on the Porch

IT HAS BEEN A JOY FOR ME to work with women all over the country as facilitator and content creator for the Christian Community Development Association's Women of Color Leadership Circle. Listening to these women's stories and re-evaluating my own journey as a leader over the past twenty-five-plus years has caused me to reflect on the challenges we face. Leadership is difficult, and despite the rewards we experience in accomplishing tasks and serving others, we also face questions and doubts. Leadership is even more complicated when race and gender are a part of the equation. How do we address issues in the workplace and use our faith as a lens to deal with bias, discrimination, and outright lack of understanding?

My journey has been filled with triumph—I started my career as a specialist and "climbed the ladder" to become a national director, yet various traumas left me doubting my abilities, worth, and belonging. I have experienced pay inequity and have been overlooked for promotions. It is in those moments we realize who God is and who we are in Christ.

Through a combination of data, my lived experiences, and the lived experiences of others, this book is designed to serve as a toolkit offering solutions, reassurance, and wisdom as you traverse your own workplace journey—after all, God's presence extends beyond the church and into the work we do. Whether we experience disappointment or mind-blowing success, at the end of the day, what we do matters. As believers, we recognize that our work should glorify God: "Whatever you do, work heartily, as for the Lord, and not for men. . . . You serve the Lord Christ" (Colossians 3:23-24).

In this book we'll lay a foundation using God's Word about our work life. Before we can address workplace and organizational culture as persons of color, we must focus on our personal growth, examining our thoughts, relationships, and emotions. It's important to understand how God sees women, so we'll draw on Scripture and the stories of people such as Deborah, Mary and Martha, Hagar, and Leah. We'll also discuss how Christ embodies leadership qualities and the importance of rest in work. Periodically we'll look at case studies based on interviews I conducted with women of color ranging in age from their late twenties to midfifties. This is an opportunity to learn from others' experiences and see how they've adapted, what lessons they've learned, and how they continue to persevere.

It is my hope that this book will provide clarity, mentoring, and even coaching to remind you that you are more than capable at succeeding no matter what space you choose to enter. You are a conqueror, and God's Word grounds you in your "why":

I can do all things through Christ, who strengthens me.
(Philippians 4:13)

Commit your deeds to Yahweh,
    and your plans shall succeed. (Proverbs 16:3)

Don't you be afraid, for I am with you.
    Don't be dismayed, for I am your God.
    I will strengthen you.
    Yes, I will help you.
    Yes, I will uphold you with the right hand of my
        righteousness. (Isaiah 41:10)

As a Christian Black woman who has been in leadership for more than three decades, I don't often see our voices represented. Secular materials don't account for faith, and Christian leadership books don't reflect my experiences as a woman or as a person of color. Books by White women may address my struggle from a gender perspective, but they fail to encapsulate my experience as a racial minority in the United States. When I wrote my dissertation I found a few texts that spoke to my circumstances, but those were filled with academic terminology and likely inaccessible to the average reader. I wanted to write something that could speak to the hearts of women like me in the many facets of life.

An overarching theme of my leadership journey has been mentorship. Without the powerful women who spoke into my life, I would not be who I am today; their generosity of time and wisdom helped plant seeds that sprouted. I am reminded of 1 Corinthians 3:6 where Paul shares that while he planted and Apollos watered, ultimately God gave the increase. Paul was instructing the church in Corinth that God uses each of us to complete his will and advance the kingdom. That church grew as a result of Paul and Apollos's stewardship, but we cannot neglect recognizing God's role in their lives.

Our experiences shape who we are, and God does not waste anything we go through. At the time of this writing I am going through a challenging season—leading an adult daughter who works for me along with a team of other young adults who are finding their way. I'm in a new role that is awkward; I am an adult child of an amazing woman who is struggling with losing her independence. My mother lives with me and our roles have changed. I find that I am leading her as she ages and needs support from me in a different way. I am leading a business, growing my clients through my work as their coach or consultant, helping them think differently about how they show up and lead others. It can be a lot at times, but I find that as I spend more time seeking God, I can carry the many loads that become heavy. This allows me to lead myself differently than I have in the past. My work with others is much more impactful and productive when I recognize where my strength comes from and who I am completely relying on.

My relationship with God didn't happen overnight. It's been a season of transitions. After being married for almost thirty years, I recently went through an amicable divorce. I moved to a new home in a new city, and shortly thereafter I left a job that represented security for me. In this difficult transition, I learned that the only stability I had in life was my relationship with God. I was blessed with some amazing friends who supported me through ambiguous moments when I wasn't sure what was next, and my mother and daughter were rocks for me, yet their encouragement and motivation could take me only so far. It was my walk with God that truly carried me.

One of the first lessons we must acknowledge as leaders is that we need God and must stay in submission under God's authority and leadership. When we move away from that, we risk believing that our judgment and experiences are all we need. The second lesson is that as leaders, we need other people. The cross is an example of leadership. It not only points up to God but it also reaches out as well. We cannot exist without God, and we definitely cannot exist without others. Leaders cannot exist in isolation.

SO WHY THE FRONT PORCH?

If leaders cannot exist in isolation, then we need spaces to gather. During my childhood, women would congregate on the front porch to converse or style each other's hair. The porch served as a space for women to share and bond. Counsel, laughter, and secrets were abundant on that front porch. This book aims to be like the front porch, providing women of color a forum to learn not just from me but from other women. It is intended to be a safe haven where we can be our authentic selves in God's and each other's company, free of judgment, and filled only with affirmation and celebration. You are blessed. You are special. You are brilliant, even when you doubt yourself or others question your capabilities—that does not alter the essence of who you are.

This book aims to offer advice and strategies like a wise friend, helping you navigate life's difficulties through applying Christian values. It is intended for all readers, because everyone exhibits leadership in some capacity, first through managing ourselves. While not all leaders guide teams, each person leads their own life. So this book strives to help anyone improve as a leader of both self and others, by imparting lessons for personal growth. I hope you will see some of your experiences reflected on these pages, and if you don't need the other lessons, just know they are there if and when you do. The front porch is always available to you.

1

What Do Leadership, Women, and Work Have to Do with It?

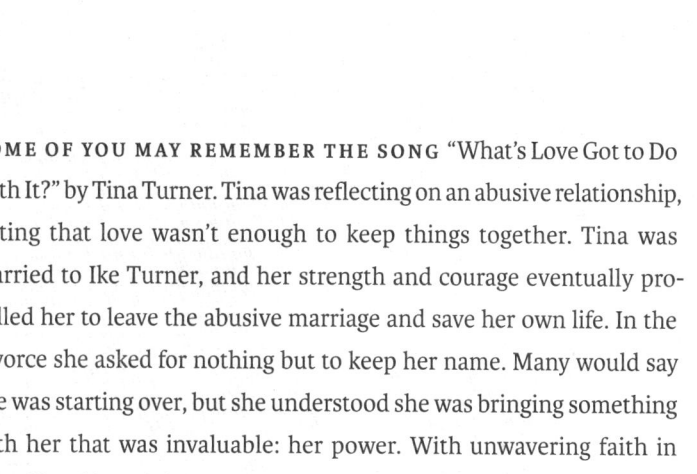

SOME OF YOU MAY REMEMBER THE SONG "What's Love Got to Do With It?" by Tina Turner. Tina was reflecting on an abusive relationship, noting that love wasn't enough to keep things together. Tina was married to Ike Turner, and her strength and courage eventually propelled her to leave the abusive marriage and save her own life. In the divorce she asked for nothing but to keep her name. Many would say she was starting over, but she understood she was bringing something with her that was invaluable: her power. With unwavering faith in herself and her abilities, she believed that her potential was limitless. Tina assessed her circumstances and aspired to a better future. She had developed a practice of reflection and tapped into her inner leader.

So what do leadership, women, and work have to do with the front porch and our faith? With a slight twist on the lyrics, we must conduct a similar examination. We must examine our thinking and interpretation of who we are and what God says about us. Many of us have grown up in faith communities that have led us to believe we are inferior to men. This misunderstanding is often rooted in the interpretation of Genesis 2:18, which states, "And Jehovah God said, It is not good that the man should be alone; I will make him a help meet for him" (ASV).

When we do not see our value in Christ, it impacts how we see ourselves in other areas of life. *Ezer kenegdo* is a Hebrew phrase that means "a helper suitable for him" and is used in the Bible to describe the relationship between Adam and Eve. *Kenegdo* says the thing God makes for Adam will be like him. So this creation will be on the same level as Adam, not better or worse. This helper will be half of a pair and will relate to Adam as the South Pole relates to the North Pole.[1] *Ezer* is also interpreted as "warrior," and *ezer kenegdo* can be interpreted as "a powerful complement." How would our lives be different if we had known earlier that we are not a "suitable helper" but were created to be a powerful complement—and that we have value to each other, to men, and to God. We must own this and walk in it. This does not minimize or diminish our brothers but recognizes our significance.

Ezer kenegdo has significant implications for women's leadership. In this context, the phrase is a powerful affirmation of women's value and potential. It suggests that women are not simply helpers or companions to men but powerful and capable leaders in their own right. This can be a powerful source of inspiration and empowerment for women who desire to lead or are currently leading. *Ezer kenegdo* can also shift the way we think about leadership. Traditionally leadership has been seen as a masculine trait; however, *ezer kenegdo* suggests that it's not about dominance or power but partnership and collaboration. This can be a helpful framework for women who want to lead in a way that is more inclusive and collaborative.

In these ways *ezer kenegdo* can help women leaders see themselves as powerful and capable and help them build strong partnerships with others, both men and women. This can help women leaders overcome the challenges they face in the workplace and achieve success in their careers.

It's important to emphasize the remarkable nature of women as God's creative masterpieces. Just like men, women are the embodiment of divine genius and are fearfully and wonderfully made. This identity as image-bearers of God is inherent and unchanging.

WOMEN MODELS IN THE BIBLE

The Bible features numerous influential women, including Deborah, Mary, Martha, Hagar, and Leah. However, many more women have made significant contributions and their stories are worth exploring. These women can teach all of us valuable lessons and inspire us in our faith journeys. I will share a few examples, but I encourage you to seek out and learn about other women in the faith who may not be as well-known.

The five daughters of Zelophehad. In Numbers 26–27, we encounter the story of the five daughters of Zelophehad: Mahlah, Noah, Hoglah, Milcah, and Tirzah. After their father died without sons, these women boldly approached Moses to request the rightful inheritance of their father's land, challenging the prevailing tradition that property immediately passed to males. Moses sought guidance from God, who affirmed that they should receive their father's land. To ensure that the inheritance remained within their tribe, the women were required to marry within the tribe, preserving their legacy and the integrity of their ancestral lineage.

Abigail. In 1 Samuel 25:3, the Bible introduces Abigail, a beautiful and intelligent woman who was married to a challenging man named Nabal. When David sought assistance from Nabal, he was met with a refusal. David's anger flared, and he planned to kill Nabal. However, Abigail intervened, displaying quick thinking and strategic reasoning to save her husband.

Her approach was calculated; she waited until daybreak, when Nabal was sober, to confront him. Abigail revealed the consequences of his actions, causing Nabal's spirit to fail, and he became like a stone. Divine retribution followed, and about ten days later, the Lord struck Nabal, leading to his death. Upon hearing of Nabal's demise, David, recognizing Abigail's wisdom and virtue, asked her to marry him (1 Samuel 25:40-42).

Priscilla. In Acts 18, we encounter the remarkable figure of Priscilla, a woman mentioned in four different biblical texts. Together with her husband, Aquila, they owned a business and dedicated their lives to supporting Paul and his ministry, becoming kingdom financiers. Priscilla's character stood out as she possessed a generous and compassionate spirit, actively involved in spreading God's word as a dedicated missionary.

Jehosheba. We are introduced to Jehoram's daughter Jehosheba, the wife of the high priest Jehoiada, in 2 Kings 11. After the assassination of King Ahaziah, his mother seized power and ruthlessly eliminated potential rivals. However, Jehosheba bravely saved her nephew, the infant Joash, keeping him hidden for six long years. When Joash was seven, she orchestrated his coronation as king. Jehosheba's courageous actions reveal her strength of character and unwavering determination.

Susanna. The Roman Catholic Bible includes the book of Susanna. Susanna was a wealthy Babylonian Jewish woman married to Jo'akim. She was the daughter of Hilki'ah and was raised to fear God. She was a stunning and devoted wife who faced a grave accusation from elders in the community who deceitfully charged her with promiscuity out of revenge for her rejection of their advances. They had a history of lying and perverting justice, abusing their power and position in the community. To further their scheme, they falsely accused her of adultery, leading to an unjust sentence of death.

Most of us are familiar with the story of Daniel, who was taken into captivity from Judah under King Nebuchadnezzar's rule and lived as an exile in Babylon. We are aware of the accounts of Daniel's faithfulness and prophetic voice, but this narrative involving Susanna isn't as well-known. Through divine intervention, God selected young Daniel to champion Susanna's defense, leading to the revelation of the elders' deception. For me, Susanna symbolizes the resilience and bravery of standing firm in the face of tremendous adversity and opposition. Her story represents standing up against power, trusting God even when your fate looks bleak.

Eunice and Lois. In 2 Timothy 1:5, Paul draws attention to Timothy's mother, Eunice, and his grandmother, Lois, emphasizing their vital role in shaping Timothy's faith. Despite the limited information available about these women, Paul emphasizes the profound impact of their training and teaching on Timothy's life. In a culture dominated by male authority, these exceptional women assumed the role of mentors, sharing wisdom that transformed Timothy's trajectory. This serves as a reminder of the influence we can have on our own children's lives, underscoring the importance of providing them with a strong foundation of faith and values.

JESUS AS THE ULTIMATE LEADERSHIP EXAMPLE

The Bible is full of female figures who exhibited exceptional leadership qualities. Let's explore what the Bible teaches us through the example of Jesus, our ultimate model of leadership.

- Jesus is a powerful leader whose impact continues well beyond his followers' earthly existence (Matthew 11:27; 28:18-20; John 17:2; Ephesians 1:20-21).
- Jesus is a servant leader who submits to God's authority (Mark 10:45).
- Jesus mentors and disciples others. He sees their potential instead of focusing solely on their problems (Matthew 28:16-20; John 8:31-38; 13:34-35).
- Jesus takes time to pray and seek God's guidance (Luke 6:12; 9:28).
- Jesus does not heal everyone he comes in contact with. He could, but he knows his assignment and who he came for (John 5:1-15).

- Jesus recognizes when power goes out of him (Luke 8:46-48). Many of us exhaust ourselves because we don't realize power leaves us daily.
- Jesus speaks truth in love (John 18:37-38).
- Jesus rests. He takes time away from the crowds (Luke 5:16).
- Jesus is enjoyable to be around. How could twelve men spend three years around someone who was constantly condemning them? They obviously want to follow him (Mark 6:7).
- Jesus is prepared for leadership as a child and is thirty when he begins his earthly ministry (Luke 2:42-47; 3:23). Leadership doesn't have to be something that happens when you're old.
- Jesus' leadership impact is immediate as the disciples multiply in number (Acts 2:47; 6:7). Leadership doesn't have to take generations to accomplish its work.
- Jesus understands that people have needs. He cares for them and makes sure their basic needs—like food and a comfortable place to sit—are met (Matthew 14:13-21; Mark 8:1-9).

Jesus is the consummate leader, and we can learn many lessons from his interactions with others. Notice the tremendous impact he made when in community, modeling behavior, mentoring, and working with the disciples and the people he encountered. Jesus' work was intentional and comprehensive, and its importance should not be lost on us.

Labor holds great significance in the eyes of God. The Bible tells us in Genesis 2:15 that God placed Adam in the Garden of Eden to work and care for it. Humans were not designed to remain idle but to fulfill a purpose. Work was not a consequence of the fall but preceded it, although Adam and Eve's sinful choices made their work more challenging.

In the book of Revelation we get a glimpse of a future where there will be a new heaven and a new earth. This world will be free from sin and all things be made new. Consequently, the nature of work will also be transformed. The apostle Paul encouraged believers to do their work before Christ's second coming with a willing spirit, as if serving the Lord directly rather than seeking recognition or reward from people. He reminded them—and us—that our ultimate reward comes from God, and we are working for Christ, the Master who will bring the inheritance of eternal life.

In the journey of life, while we secure financial stability and pursue purpose, it is imperative that we seek divine favor and establish our work with God's guidance. Jesus' servant leadership is how we as Christians and women of color can live out being e*zer kenegdo* today.

SCRIPTURES TO CONSIDER

The hands of the diligent ones shall rule,
> but laziness ends in slave labor. (Proverbs 12:24)

In all hard work there is profit,
> but the talk of the lips leads only to poverty. (Proverbs 14:23)

Commit your deeds to Yahweh,
> and your plans shall succeed. (Proverbs 16:3)

It shall not be so among you; but whoever desires to become great among you shall be your servant. Whoever desires to be first among you shall be your bondservant, even as the Son of Man came not to be served, but to serve, and to give his life as a ransom for many. (Matthew 20:26-28)

To whomever much is given, of him will much be required; and to whom much was entrusted, of him more will be asked. (Luke 12:48)

Doing nothing through rivalry or through conceit, but in humility, each counting others better than himself; each of you not just looking to his own things, but each of you also to the things of others. (Philippians 2:3-4)

QUESTIONS FOR REFLECTION

1. How does the meaning of *ezer kenegdo* resonate with you? In what ways are you a warrior?
2. What is God saying to you about your leadership journey through the stories of women in the Bible?
3. Does Jesus' leadership example help you find purpose in your work? Why or why not?

PRAYER

Dear Lord, I am grateful for revealing the significance of women in the Scriptures to me. I am confident there is a divine purpose for my life and the work I am called to do. I ask you to empower me to make a positive impact on the world. Grant me the strength to serve others, lead with wisdom and compassion, and live a life that brings honor and glory to your name. In the precious name of Jesus, amen.

2

What Does the Data Say?

I'VE OFTEN HEARD THE EXPRESSION that men lie, and women lie, but numbers don't lie. Data is often used to tell a story, to paint a picture. Data can inform our decision-making, validate personal narratives, and help us create sound strategy. Yet numbers can also be misleading. If one out of four people is suffering from an issue, we tend to focus on the one (and we should). Yet there are three others we need to learn from as well—why is the issue not affecting them?

Data can offer a bleak picture without helping us understand the barriers that create the situation, and we can easily misinterpret the numbers. When we don't address structural and societal barriers, we can make assumptions about communities of color that are not accurate. These barriers can include education, income, lack of support networks, and advocacy. If data does not recognize those barriers, we are not telling the real story of what our communities face.

For many of us, the numbers in this chapter reflect our lived experience. If you are a woman of color, you likely won't be shocked by the information to come. It highlights the progress our communities have made, but it also shows how far we still need to go. The purpose of sharing this data is to emphasize why we need supportive communities and tactics to persevere in difficult environments. Regardless of whether we are in corporate America, nonprofit leadership, or government, we all face problems that call on our vigor, intelligence, and consideration. While not exhaustive, this data invites us to understand why our collective voices are so critical.

I don't think we realize how many of us exist collectively as women of color. Note the following:

- In 2021, 20.3 percent of the population consisted of women of color.
- By 2060, the majority of women in this country will be women of color.
- Asian women and Latinas will make up a significant portion of the workforce by 2030.[1]

As I was researching this chapter, I was blown away by the sheer numbers that exist and their implications for our collective power as a group. For so long we have been "othered" because of our race, gender, or other identities. This is an opportunity for us as a group to begin to think strategically about ways we can connect and work together more consistently. We need each other, and I am encouraged by some of the solidarity I am witnessing in today's political environment. Women of color must join together to express our concerns and collaborate. This type of collective action is critical as we plan how we can use our power for the benefit of all.

I have also witnessed that our lack of intentionality can create harm as well. We must be aware of the divide-and-conquer tactics that pit us against one another, instead seeking to understand and work together to solve issues that affect our communities. We are more powerful together than we are apart.

Maslow's hierarchy of needs is a great tool to remind us of what we require in order to succeed.[2] Things like food, water, air, safety, belonging and love, and esteem all contribute to our ability to reach self-actualization or the realization of our full potential. When we are not fulfilling our God-given potential, we miss out, whether we realize it or not. We need each other to walk in the fullness of our callings and purpose because when one of us is great, we all benefit!

Despite the population growth of women of color, we still have obstacles to overcome. Although we have witnessed women of color take on roles that were previously unattainable, the ceiling is real for women of color. In addition to the limited number of women of color who obtain C-level roles or serve on corporate boards, we also have the highest unemployment rate.[3] Race and gender often forecast economic status, education, health, living conditions, job prospects, and overall welfare more accurately than other factors. As leaders, we would be remiss not to recognize how racial identity and gender shape us and our communities.

NONPROFIT MANAGEMENT

Those of us in nonprofit spaces are fully aware of the challenges that exist in staffing. Many organizations serve communities of color but fail to have representation in leadership. One of the most eye-opening reports that affirms the absence of women of color in nonprofit leadership spaces is the Race to Lead series, an initiative of the Building Movement Project in which more than twelve thousand people have been surveyed in 2016, 2019, and 2022. The series offers data on nonprofit leaders of color across the country, and the research affirms that most organizations have predominantly White boards and leadership teams but are more diverse at the staff and community level.[4] In their Women of Color report they found that racial and gender bias prevented women of color from advancing in nonprofit management. Despite having advanced degrees, women of color were frequently overlooked for high-level leadership positions. The researchers also found that women of color faced greater scrutiny, received less recognition, and were paid less than others.[5]

As a Black woman who has served in nonprofit management in a variety of roles, I know that the disparities are real. I've experienced them. I remember being laid off from a role in the late 2000s. White colleagues were allowed to remain with the organization while all the women of color were let go from staff and contractor roles. After that position ended, I applied for numerous positions only to be told I was overqualified. I witnessed women of color who were significantly more qualified than their counterparts not promoted. I have been underpaid compared to White male colleagues with less education and experience. The data validates our experiences, but too many of us have anecdotal experiences that affirm what the statistics relate.

CORPORATE AMERICA

Things are not much different in corporate America. Women of color make up just 3% of C-suite positions.[6] McKinsey's 2023 Women in the Workplace report reveals that the rate of women of color being promoted to manager roles has dropped from 82 per 100 to 73 per 100. The report also shows that Black women and Asian women both deal with being mistaken for someone else of the same race.[7] Women of color hold only 7.8% of all corporate board seats.[8] It's very difficult for women of color to even access corporate board positions. There are several services that create connections to these opportunities, but many seek exorbitant fees. Often it is relationships and networks that lead to these appointments. If we are not in these spaces, we have difficulty even finding out about them. I'm grateful for entities like the Forté Foundation and 50/50 Women on Boards that help connect women to corporate board roles, but the opportunities are few and far between.

Black women are making strides in several nontraditional industries that have been dominated by men, such as sports. Cynthia Marshall was the first Black female CEO in NBA history. "Cynt" Marshall, CEO of the Dallas Mavericks, announced her retirement effective at the end of 2024. She will remain a consultant through 2025, but her departure from this role was quite a loss, considering that there are no other Black women CEOs or presidents of NBA teams. Sandra Douglass Morgan became the president of the Las Vegas Raiders in 2022 and is the first Black woman president of an NFL team.[9] These firsts are still happening for Black women and other women of color.

I wrote an article for the *Dallas Morning News* to celebrate Cynt's impact and discovered that "10.4% of Fortune 500 companies are run by women. At one time there were three Black women in this statistic—Thasunda Brown Duckett, CEO of TIAA; Toni Townes-Whitley, CEO of SAIC, and previously Rosalind Brewer, CEO of Walgreens Boots Alliance, who stepped down in 2023 after leading an S&P 500 company. Before Brewer, Ursula Burns was the last Black woman to command an S&P 500 company after stepping down from Xerox in 2016."[10]

This narrative is not unique to Black women. Latinas are dealing with similar experiences in both corporate America and in sports. Sadly, only three Latinas have been the CEO of a Fortune 500 company. In 2017, Geisha Williams was the first Latina CEO of a Fortune 500 company, PG&E. She stepped down in 2019.[11] Cheryl Miller led AutoNation from 2019–2022.[12] At this writing, the only Latina CEO of a Fortune 500 company is Priscilla Almodovar, the CEO of Fannie Mae, who began in 2022.[13]

Latinas and Asian American women are experiencing a number of firsts in sports as well. In 2013, Dorene Dominguez became the first Latina minority owner of an NBA team, the Sacramento Kings.[14] The statistics for Asian American women are also dismal. Kim Ng was the general manager of the Miami Marlins and left that role in 2023.[15] Natalie Nakase was the first Asian American woman to serve as head coach of the WNBA in 2024.[16]

The data on Indigenous women in leadership as CEOs of Fortune 500 companies is limited, but there are women shattering stereotypes in male-dominated fields. Stephanie A. Bryan was elected in 2014 as the Tribal Chair and CEO for the Poarch Creek Indians. Karlene Hunter started Native American Natural Foods in 2006 and as a member of the Oglala Sioux tribe, she has been recognized for her work with awards from the Small Business Association and the Specialty Food Association. Lacey Horn is the CEO of Native Advisory, focused on helping tribal leaders with financial consulting, and runs a cryptocurrency firm as well. She is a member of the Cherokee Nation and as the former treasurer for the nation, she ran a "$1.2 billion annual budget and negotiated a $170 million loan to enlarge health care options" for Indigenous people.[17]

As I child, I remember hearing the expression that it is lonely at the top, and this emphasizes that even with the advancements that are being made as we enter new terrain, we are often the only ones. Rising through the ranks is an important feat, especially when marked by significant obstacles and a lack of colleagues that can offer understanding and support.

GOVERNMENT

As we explore the advancement of women to political office, it's encouraging to see that strides have been made, but there is still work to be done. Kamala Harris is the first woman of color to serve as vice president of the United States, but according to the Pew Research Center's 2023 report, there were just sixty-one women of color serving as voting or nonvoting members in the 118th Congress. Slightly less than half of them (twenty-nine) were Black, twenty were Latina, and eleven were Asian American.[18] The organization Win with Black Women has more than ninety thousand Black women involved with the goal of building advocacy and political power. Vote, Run, Lead is another group dedicated to increasing the number of women in politics because of the need for representation.

After all, representation matters. As children we picture ourselves in jobs based on what we see and are aware of. Growing up I was always told that federal jobs were worth aspiring to because they protected those of us from diverse backgrounds. For many of us, these were the "good jobs." These were the jobs where we could experience longevity, increased opportunity for growth, and retirement with a great pension. Yet the dream job in the federal government isn't always perfect for women of color: Native, Asian, Black, and Latina women were all found to earn less than average in federal jobs. In addition, resignations and involuntary separations are higher for these groups as well.[19]

THE MINISTRY AND CLERGY

The challenge is not just in philanthropy, corporate America, or government. The church has not been the most welcoming place for women of color in leadership either. When I was growing up, women could not speak from the pulpit in church. They were relegated to teaching Sunday school or working in the children's ministry. I never saw a woman in a clergy role until I was an adult in my midtwenties and had my first female pastor, a Black woman. It totally changed my paradigm. Yet I remember hearing her discuss the bias she experienced not just from men but from Black men. She was not invited to some churches. She was told by one man that she could not teach him because she had a monthly period. That's been almost thirty years ago, and I know more women ministers who are serving in local congregations, yet the challenges they face are still very real.

In the article "Gender and Race in Ministry Leadership: Experiences of Black Clergywomen," the authors note there has been growth in Black women attending seminary, but disrespect still exists because of gender and racial bias from men in ministry.[20] Women of color make up only 4% of the United Methodist Church clergy, although there has been an increase in women of color serving as elders in the church.[21] The report "The State of Clergywomen in the US: A Statistical Update" provides a glimpse of the advances and challenges of women in ministry. According to the report, 80% of lay ministers in the Catholic church are women, and there have been increases in women in ministry in various denominations such as the AME church.[22]

No matter the industry, women of color face similar challenges. Know that you are not alone, and there are many women experiencing similar victories and challenges daily.

THE BACKLASH IS REAL

In President Biden's first day in office, he signed an executive order titled Advancing Racial Equity and Support for Underserved Communities Through the Federal Government. Shortly afterward, the backlash began. The *American Alliance for Equal Rights v. Fearless Fund* court case sued the Fearless Fund, which offered $20,000 grants to Black women business owners, but an appeals court ruled these charitable donations to be discriminatory.[23] States such as Texas and Florida created legislation to eradicate DEI (diversity, equity, and inclusion) from education and the workplace. Dozens of other states have passed more than one hundred bills to regulate or restrict DEI programs.[24] After George Floyd's murder in 2020, corporations pledged more than $300 billion to support racial equity,[25] but many have reneged on their pledges, and many in DEI roles—especially women of color—found their positions eliminated.[26]

The backlash we are experiencing is real. We cannot change the data or the legalities overnight, but there are things we can do. How do we protect ourselves in the midst of such turmoil and confusion?

A POSSIBLE SOLUTION: THE PAST CAN BE A PRESENT

I was blessed to witness some amazing women whose shoulders I stand on today. My grandmother, Thelma Gilyard Pinkney, is one of those women. My grandmother was born in 1921, a time when the opportunities for women of color were limited. My grandmother had only a sixth grade education, but she was one of the smartest people I ever met. She married my grandfather and had five children. With a limited education, she became a housekeeper for a local physician. My grandmother's life taught me a lot of lessons that we can use in moments like these:

- Her faith was her fuel. Despite the limitations life presented, my grandmother leaned on her belief in God.
- She took care of herself. My grandmother was very mindful about what she ate, the people she spent time around, and the stress she carried. She did not allow messy surroundings, and she didn't deal with messy people. She made sure as much as possible to experience the peace promised by God.
- Thelma was a lifelong learner. She did not allow the world's definition of education to define her and she continued reading and growing. As a child, I read all the magazines she brought from Dr. Rushing's home—after she finished with them!
- She did not allow the conditions of the world to dictate how she felt or how she used her gifts. My grandmother was one of the most stylish women I have known. She would see an outfit on television she liked, make a pattern from newspapers, and sew the clothing herself. Nothing was too difficult for her to make if she wanted it. Even in her late seventies, she came to slay!

My grandmother lived in a different era with different expectations than we have today, but we can glean much from our ancestors who paved the way with their courage and determination. They didn't have some of the tools that we have, which means we can take those things from them that help our journey and add what we need for our context. Just like my grandmother didn't allow others' beliefs to define her, we can refuse to allow the data to define our trajectories. The past can be a gift to us when we examine how our ancestors dealt with atrocities and still found ways to embody joy.

SCRIPTURES TO CONSIDER

> And whatever you do, work heartily, as for the Lord, and not for men. (Colossians 3:23)

> Let the favor of the Lord our God be on us.
> Establish the work of our hands for us.
> Yes, establish the work of our hands. (Psalm 90:17)

QUESTIONS FOR REFLECTION

1. What does the data say about your industry?
2. Are you surprised by what you read? Why or why not?
3. How will you use this data moving forward in your journey?

PRAYER

Heavenly Father, we are grateful for the blessing of employment. Thank you for bestowing on each of us unique abilities, imagination, and brilliance. As we progress in our vocations and understanding, guide us on our journey. I have faith that you are directing my footsteps and illuminating the road ahead. I am confident that you have only the finest things intended for me and that you cherish me. I know that even better things await as I follow your will and heed your words. In the name of Jesus Christ, amen.

3

You Are Not an Impostor

ON THE FIRST DAY OF MY PHD PROGRAM, I felt like an outsider among my intelligent and accomplished cohort members. It wasn't that I was the only Black person or woman in the group. As I listened to others share about their accomplishments, I didn't feel that mine were on par. I felt out of my league: I was from Louisiana living in Texas and there was no one else in the cohort from the Deep South. I didn't speak as they did and my life experiences were totally different. I was Christian, while many of them were not believers and some were atheists.

Impostor syndrome gripped me, and I secretly feared that the program directors would discover their mistake in admitting me. I remember waiting for a faculty member to tap me on the shoulder to let me know they'd made a mistake. Can you believe that at that juncture in my life I still felt as if I didn't belong? When I have shared my story, this feeling of inadequacy has resonated with others, especially women. Many of us struggle daily, questioning our worthiness and place in our respective endeavors.

The impostor phenomenon, commonly experienced by high-achieving women, is a concept developed by Pauline Rose Clance and Suzanne Imes in their groundbreaking research in the late 1970s.[1] Working with over 150 successful women, Clance and Imes observed similar characteristics. Notably, these women often attributed their achievements to external circumstances, downplaying their own internal abilities, knowledge, and skills.

For women of color, feeling like an impostor is compounded by issues of race and gender. A study conducted by the University of Texas at Austin sampled 106 African Americans, 102 Asian Americans, and 108 Latino/a Americans. The researchers found that African American and Asian students with high impostor feelings experienced anxiety and depression due to discrimination and racism.[2]

The study's findings for Latino/a students are surprising, possibly due to cultural factors. Latino/a students with low impostor syndrome feelings were more inclined to adopt a pessimistic mindset, leading them to give up personal control because they believed they couldn't influence others' perceptions of them. For Latino/a students, high impostor feelings positively predicted anxiety, but low impostor feelings worsened the effects of perceived discrimination on depression and anxiety.

A more recent study characterizes the impostor phenomenon (or impostor syndrome, as it's come to be known popularly) as a psychological experience wherein individuals doubt their abilities and achievements despite evidence of success.[3] Affected individuals cannot internalize their achievements, leading to pervasive feelings of self-doubt, anxiety, depression, and fear of being exposed as a fraud in their work. Some overprepare or procrastinate when faced with a task or deadline in a pattern known as the impostor cycle. This behavior involves either going above and beyond to prove one's worth or waiting until the last minute to complete the work. Both are driven by the fear of being "found out" as incompetent. Even when success is experienced, it's short-lived.

This research illuminates the profound impact our narratives have on our self-perception. Throughout our lives, particularly as girls, we face constant comparisons and pressure to demonstrate our worth, and this shapes our identities.

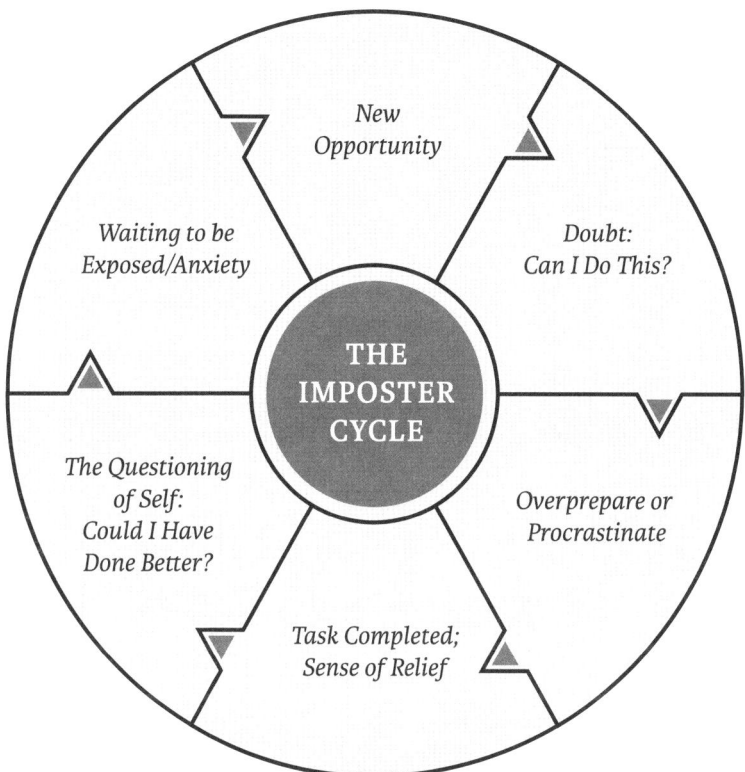

ORIGINS OF THE IMPOSTOR SYNDROME

Clance and Imes identify two groups of "impostors" in early family histories. The first group consists of women who grew up with a sibling or close relative deemed the "intelligent" family member, while they themselves were seen as "sensitive" or "the social one." The implied message was that their intellectual achievements would never measure up. This created an internal conflict, with one part of these women believing the family myth and the other longing to prove it wrong. School presented an opportunity to prove their intelligence. Success through excellent grades, academic honors, and praise from teachers boosted their self-esteem and sparked hope for recognition beyond the "sensitive" or "charming" label.

Consequently, these women often seek external validation, harboring the internalized belief that they are inadequate and intensifying their efforts will enable them to fit in. Their self-worth becomes inextricably linked to their actions rather than their intrinsic qualities. This pattern becomes even more convoluted for girls of color. Research shows that Black girls are treated as older than they actually are and that they're punished more in school as early as five years old: "Teachers, and even parents, may expect black girls to exceed age-appropriate levels of responsibility at home or assume they don't need to be comforted after emotionally distressing events."[4] It's difficult enough being young and trying to figure out our place in the world. The added complication of facing higher expectations as children can affect the way we see ourselves and how we "fit" in the world. It's a juggling act for women of color, and this act starts early in life.

In an alternative explanation for the origin of the impostor phenomenon, Clance and Imes point to families that focus constantly on a girl's exceptional abilities and impeccable nature. This reinforcement instills in the girl the belief that she can achieve anything she sets her mind to without effort and that she is inherently superior. The family shares anecdotes from her early childhood, such as her rapid language development and ease with nursery rhymes, further solidifying this belief. Within her family, the girl is perceived as flawless.

As she matures, challenges and difficulties disrupt the illusion of effortless perfection she once exhibited. The gap between her perceived abilities and her real-life experiences generates a sense of unease. Despite this, she feels compelled to uphold the expectations imposed by her family, although she recognizes deep down that sustaining the façade of perfection could result in exposure.

During childhood, many of us internalize narratives and beliefs that shape our self-perception. In this scenario, the girl begins to question her parents' beliefs and doubt her abilities, highlighting how our childhood experiences can lead to a sense of inadequacy. It is important to reflect on our personal journey and identify when we began questioning ourselves, our abilities, and our intellect. Often, the seeds of these doubts are planted in childhood and adolescence, shaping our self-perception in significant ways.

CHARACTERISTICS OF IMPOSTOR SYNDROME

There are five characteristics women experience when experiencing the impostor phenomenon, according to Clance and Imes. Let's look at these in turn.

Perfectionism. Perfectionism involves setting excessively high and unrealistic standards for oneself, often leading to self-criticism and a fear of making mistakes. This mindset can hinder individuals from pursuing opportunities or making decisions due to a belief that they do not meet the required criteria or an overwhelming need for analysis, resulting in "analysis paralysis."

Atychiphobia. While perfectionists strive to perform every task flawlessly, those who experience atychiphobia are preoccupied with the potential for failure and concentrate on the worst possible outcomes. During my childhood, I recall the pervasive influence of Murphy's Law, which suggests that "anything that can go wrong will." It seemed like the more I thought about it, the more Murphy's Law was in effect! Atychiphobia can be intensified for women of color when they have experienced significant rejection or criticism, especially in the workplace.

Competence denial. Humility is a core value of the Christian faith. As Christians, many of us tend to downplay our skills and abilities because we believe acknowledging them shows a lack of humility. But this inclination to undervalue our knowledge and abilities, known as competence denial, is a type of self-devaluation.

As Christian women of color, we often lessen ourselves so that others feel comfortable, and we equate this with humility. But humility is a state of being free from pride or arrogance, and we must beware falling into the trap of false humility. This "humble-bragging" involves deflecting genuine praise while at the same time seeking compliments to draw attention to ourselves. It manifests when we talk excessively about our humility, falsely portray ourselves as helpless or lacking power, and employ self-deprecating humor. In doing this we invalidate who we are and who God created us to be.

The challenge lies in achieving a harmonious balance between confidence and humility. We must avoid becoming overly self-absorbed and take care not to mistake arrogance for genuine confidence. A wise friend of mine once said, "Arrogance stems from attempting to persuade others, while confidence emerges from a deep-seated belief in one's own identity."

True humility involves a balanced self-awareness in which we honestly acknowledge both our strengths and weaknesses. It allows us to celebrate others' successes without feeling diminished, and it helps us avoid self-deprecation, the tendency to belittle ourselves to boost others' self-esteem. Instead of adopting an inflated sense of self or undervaluing ourselves or others, let's acknowledge our own worth while recognizing and respecting the value of others. Marianne Williamson reminds us that shining our light brightly gives others permission to do the same:

> Our deepest fear is not that we are inadequate. Our deepest fear is that we are powerful beyond measure. It is our light, not our darkness, that most frightens us. We ask ourselves, "Who am I to be brilliant, gorgeous, talented, fabulous?" Actually, who are you not to be? You are a child of God. Your playing small does not serve the world. There is nothing enlightened about shrinking so that other people won't feel insecure around you. We are all meant to shine, as children do. We were born to make manifest the glory of God that is within us. It's not just in some of us; it's in everyone. And as we let our own light shine, we unconsciously give other people permission to do the same. As we are liberated from our own fear, our presence automatically liberates others.[5]

Achievemephobia. Alongside the fear of failure exists a lesser-known phenomenon: achievemephobia, or the fear of success. The prospect of being in the spotlight and facing potential criticism in a cancel-culture society can be daunting, prompting individuals to opt for a more subdued existence. This fear of success can manifest as procrastination, setting low goals, or engaging in self-destructive behaviors to avoid pressure and expectations. Athletes and performers frequently experience apprehension regarding their ability to maintain their current level of achievement. They feel pressure to surpass records set by others or to match or exceed their own top performances to meet the expectations of fans and the media. In the workplace, the pressure to maintain excellence can be overwhelming. After receiving outstanding evaluations or reviews, some individuals may find it tempting to adopt a low-key approach to avoid the increased expectations that come with recognition.

Superheroism. The defining characteristic of superheroism is the pursuit of excellence to an unhealthy degree. Women of color feel pressure to excel in all aspects of life, which amplifies their sense of superheroism. In Zora Neale Hurston's *Their Eyes Were Watching God*, Janie Crawford says, "Black women are the mules of the earth"—a statement that exemplifies the archetype of the Strong Black Woman. Many women of color might as well bear an "S" on their chests. This archetype perpetuates the belief that women of color derive their value from their tireless efforts.

As a college student I read Michelle Wallace's *Black Macho and the Myth of the Superwoman* (1979), which explores the challenges Black women faced during and after the 1960s civil rights movement. Wallace faced opposition in sharing Black women's challenges as they sought to be valued and viewed as equal, but she laid the groundwork for further exploration of the superhero concept many struggle with.

One of those who carried on this work was Dr. Cheryl L. Woods-Giscombé, who introduced the concept of Black superwoman syndrome. This schema consists of five characteristics:[6]

- An internalized sense of having to project a façade of strength
- A perceived need to suppress emotional expression
- Reluctance to display vulnerability and seek support from others
- Determination to succeed despite limited resources
- A tendency to prioritize caregiving responsibilities over self-care

In communities of color, we have watched our mothers and other women embrace strength as a badge of honor—to their demise. We have been taught that asking for help is weakness, and this has not served us well. In being strong and creating a narrative that everything is okay, we are not sharing our truth.

I was guilty of this some years ago. When working at a large nonprofit I had a limited budget and no staff support. I was determined to prove I could do the job so they would give me the resources I needed. But a friend reminded me that if I did so well without resources, why would they give me what I needed? I was killing myself to prove my worth while others ran departments that had less work, teams to help, and bigger budgets. I was ensuring that those I was assisting had what they needed, but I was not prioritizing what I needed professionally to be successful.

That role taught me a lot about organizations that use you up and demand more if you don't speak up and advocate for what you need. I learned quickly that I deserved more! For many women of color, we are on a constant roller coaster trying to prove our value, hoping we'll be seen and our worth will be validated.

WOMEN OF COLOR AND IMPOSTOR SYNDROME

While Black women are frequently praised for their resilience, the circumstances that necessitate this strength are too often ignored. Being expected to excel in all aspects of life, both at home and at work, has implications for our mental and physical health.

The media's portrayal of Black women further exacerbates our feelings of inadequacy and perpetuates impostor syndrome. According to the

Geena Davis Institute on Gender and Media, Black women in family films are more likely to be depicted without an occupation compared with their counterparts in family TV shows (39.6% vs. 10.4%).[7] According to Puente, media depictions of Latinas significantly influence how people view Latinas in their daily lives.[8] They are often portrayed as "extremely loud and obnoxious" and not in professional positions.[9] A study conducted by Mukkamala and Suyemoto found that Asian American women are perceived as successful and intelligent but lacking leadership ability, ignoring discrimination, devoid of agency and initiative, and often working as maids or in other service-related roles.[10] The trope for Indigenous women is the need to be saved and then taught how to assimilate. Plus, "when Native female characters are not supporting the White, male protagonist, they are often being brutalized." Even more often, Native women are invisible, replaced by White women in many roles.[11]

It is common for women of color to invest significant effort in challenging prevailing stereotypes. As a child, I was told I needed to exert ten times more effort than others based on the assumption that I started at a disadvantage. Societal pressure of this nature amplifies our feelings of inadequacy and self-doubt, contributing to the formation of narratives that influence our self-perception and behavior in the workplace.

In response to the notion of impostor syndrome for women of color, a recent Harvard Business Review presents a counterargument.[12] The idea that this phenomenon is a clinical diagnosis is problematic, according to the authors, because its development in the 1970s neglected to consider the effects of systemic racism, classism, xenophobia, and other prejudices. The article argues that the concept of impostor syndrome medicalized a common experience in the workplace—particularly for women of color—of mild anxiety, self-doubt, and discomfort. Instead of concentrating on isolated solutions, the key is to foster an environment that values and embraces different leadership styles and perspectives. This involves recognizing and treating racial, ethnic, and gender identities as equally valid and professional.

The authors assert that the determination of who is considered "professional" is influenced by cultural biases and prejudices. They emphasize that the presence of marginalized individuals in certain spaces is a consequence of persistent activism and reluctantly implemented legislation. The authors suggest that rather than scrutinizing individuals, the focus should be on examining and addressing the environments that engender these feelings of exclusion.

Growing up, I would often hear the behavior of people of color disparagingly compared to "crabs in a bucket," where the crabs collectively pull down any individual trying to climb out. This behavior hinders the crabs' cooperation and their ability to escape a non-native environment such as a bucket. Rather than blaming the crabs, we should investigate the underlying reasons for their actions. Could it be that their behavior is a result of the trauma they experience being confined in an unsuitable environment? This is a sobering reminder of the power of narrative and the advantages enjoyed by those who can communicate their perspectives effectively. The crabs would likely have a vastly different interpretation of their experience.

WHAT DOES GOD SAY ABOUT *YOU*?

With an expanding understanding of myself and God's perspective, I came to realize that self-doubt was a detrimental mindset. It was imperative for me to shift away from this mentality, as it hindered both personal and interpersonal growth.

Many of us have internalized negative beliefs about ourselves, attributing our shortcomings to personal inadequacies rather than recognizing that our surroundings have shaped our self-worth. We must find our true validation in God. As 2 Corinthians 3:5 states, "Not that we are sufficient of ourselves, to account anything as from ourselves; but our sufficiency is from God." We must acknowledge God as the source of the gifts and talents we are blessed with. Our endeavors, whether fulfilling our purpose or guiding others, are rooted in God's power and preparation.

In the Bible we read of numerous individuals who were called by God despite feeling inadequate. One example is Moses, portrayed in Exodus 4:1-17. When God instructs Moses to lead the Israelites out of Egypt, Moses expresses doubts and concerns. He worries that the Israelites will not listen to him or believe him and he questions his ability as a speaker, feeling he is slow and hesitant.

In response, God reminds Moses that he is the giver of sight, hearing, and speech and that he will provide assistance. God assures Moses that he will help him speak and tell him what to say. However, Moses remains reluctant and begs God to send someone else. This angers the Lord, who tells Moses that his brother Aaron, a skilled speaker, is approaching and will be glad to see him.

Despite God's calling, Moses harbors self-doubt, believing that his brother Aaron possesses superior abilities. Many of us, like Moses, question God's plan for us and the opportunities that come our way. Instead of relying on our own strength and the opinions of others, we should recognize that God has the power to bring success through us. With God, anything is possible (Matthew 19:26), and we can achieve overwhelming victory through Christ's love (Romans 8:37). We should stop turning down opportunities meant for us out of self-doubt.

In spaces where conformity is demanded, it becomes easy to feel overwhelmed and mentally taxed. But remember that God does not expect us to mold ourselves to the world's standards. Our individuality and distinctions are assets, even when the world tries to convince us otherwise. It is crucial to reaffirm our identity and our connection to Jesus. By tapping into the strength of our faith, we can persevere and speak our truth boldly in the face of authority.

You are not a mere imitator but a unique creation, made in the divine image of God. Within you lies a treasure trove of gifts and talents, each a reflection of your extraordinary purpose. Embrace this truth and embark on a journey of self-discovery, seeking God's guidance and wisdom to illuminate your path. It is time to step boldly into the destiny that awaits you, knowing you are equipped for greatness.

In four years, I graduated with my PhD from Antioch University while working full time, supervising a team across the country, working in senior leadership, being married, and raising a preteen daughter. If anything, the PhD taught me that with God, all things are possible. To say the experience was easy would be deceptive, but it was life-changing. It not only stretched me professionally, but it taught me that I am capable when I believe in myself.

I saw God's hand throughout the process as he used that experience to build my faith and love walk. For the first time in my life, I was in rooms with people who held dramatically different beliefs than my own, and instead of being reserved, I took the opportunity to dig deeper, to learn more about them. In doing so I gained learning that a degree could not provide. I started out believing I didn't belong, and not only did I graduate, but I now sit on the board of governors for the Antioch University system.

Won't God do it? If you just believe . . .

SCRIPTURES TO CONSIDER

> I can do all things through Christ, who strengthens me. (Philippians 4:13)

> For we are his workmanship, created in Christ Jesus for good works, which God prepared before that we would walk in them. (Ephesians 2:10)

> Before I formed you in the womb I knew you,
> and before you were born I consecrated you;
> I appointed you a prophet to the nations. (Jeremiah 1:5 ESV)

QUESTIONS FOR REFLECTION

1. Reflect on a time when you felt inadequate or like you didn't belong. How did you address your feelings?
2. Consider the strengths and abilities you possess and how you can apply them in a leadership role.
3. Are there ways for you to grow in self-assurance concerning your skills and competencies? If so, what specific actions can you take?

PRAYER

God, you have crafted my existence with a profound purpose and a meticulously planned path. Every aspect of my being is intentional and guided by your wisdom. Even in a world that may not recognize my potential, you have ordained me to contribute meaningfully to your kingdom. Your word assures me that if I seek wisdom, you will abundantly bestow it upon me. Please continue to illuminate my path, guiding my steps with unwavering clarity. Do not allow my insecurities to hinder me from embracing all you have lovingly designed for me. In the precious name of Jesus, amen.

PROFILES IN LEADERSHIP

You Are *Not* an Impostor: Serita's Story

Serita is a Black woman in her early forties and the founder of a powerfully effective nonprofit organization that addresses health disparities. She was a retail manager and arts instructor before stepping out in faith to launch the nonprofit.

One of the most challenging situations Serita has faced in the workplace has been being taken advantage of as a result of her people-pleasing tendencies. She experienced betrayal and deception from those she trusted, but instead of allowing this to define her, Serita chose to see it as a learning experience that strengthens her team as they continue to refine processes and organizational culture.

Serita initially believed that race had not had a significant impact on her career, but she acknowledges now that she was blind to many microaggressions and biases. Her activism, particularly her support of Black women and Black lives, has led to some adversity. However, she has found a supportive community among like-minded organizations and feels grateful for their solidarity.

Despite the fact that she leads a thriving organization with a multi-million-dollar budget, Serita has dealt with impostor syndrome and lack of confidence. She emphasizes that women of color in leadership need to recognize their achievements and believe in themselves, as she herself is learning to do. Serita is coming to trust her abilities and make decisions independently rather than always seeking others' input. In order to grow in leadership, she has focused on healing and forgiveness, which has assisted in building her confidence.

Serita feels challenged by her lack of previous CEO experience but is committed to ongoing learning. She continues to work through impostor syndrome, feeling that others on her team may believe in her more than she believes in herself. As the CEO of a large organization, she wears many hats and finds it challenging to know when to delegate responsibilities to others.

Serita's faith is an important component of her life and has shaped her perspective on workplace policies and practices. Her organization operates on a thirty-two-hour workweek and offers comprehensive health care and competitive salaries. Rooted in her faith practice, these policies create a more just and sustainable workplace. Serita sees her leadership role as one of service to others and ensuring that everyone earns a livable wage.

Serita believes that sensitivity to criticism is a strength rather than a weakness, and she prioritizes creating spaces of authenticity in the workplace and in life. Her beliefs are a result of her unconventional background, including struggles in school and a nontraditional path to leadership. Her unique perspective and experiences have led her to build her organization that is inclusive and supportive.

Lessons for Younger Women

- Stay true to yourself and view challenging situations as opportunities for growth and refinement.
- Be authentic in dealing with cultural expectations in corporate America.
- Create spaces of authenticity. It's important to find ways to be yourself and be accepted.

4

Who You Need in Life

DURING MY HIGH SCHOOL YEARS, I encountered an incredible woman, Sharon S., who played a pivotal role in shaping my life. An adviser for student government, this woman had a genuine interest in my well-being and an unwavering belief in my leadership potential. I am eternally grateful for the positive influence she had on my life. This experience motivated me to become a guiding force for other women of color who need the same support and encouragement I yearned for during my formative years.

When I was starting out in my career, another experience also left a deep impression on me. I sought guidance from a successful woman in the nonprofit sector, Shari W., hoping to learn from her expertise. I arranged appointments with her administrative assistant, but to my dismay, she was consistently absent when I arrived. This happened several times, leaving me feeling undervalued and unimportant. This experience inspired me to make a difference for young women by offering the support and mentorship I had desired but did not receive.

Several years later I had an opportunity to put this idea into action. During a gathering of ministry, business, and nonprofit leaders, a young man approached and said his friend wanted to meet me. Bemnet, a college student, told me she'd been inspired by my work and aspired to a similar path. Recognizing the importance of nurturing young talent, I made time for her and provided her with a volunteer opportunity that eventually led to a job. Our professional relationship continued for six years, during which Bemnet became my administrative assistant. After I left that role, she accepted a position with me at the State Fair of Texas. I have been immensely grateful for Bemnet's dedication and hard work. Now she is vice president at Girl Scouts of Northeast Texas, and I am fortunate to have the opportunity to collaborate with her as a consultant. Our professional journey together has been mutually enriching, as we have both learned from one another. My life is richer because she has been in it.

Even at my age and at this stage in life, I recognize the importance of a village around me that speaks into my life. I am thankful for the women who have mentored and taught me, such as Michele, my first boss after college. Michele played a pivotal role in opening doors and also demonstrated the significance of strong relationships. For example, at one point she had me work with Latino students while my Latina colleague, Rita, focused on working with Black students. At the time I didn't understand why this was important, but I now know that students of color need to see other people of color who care for them.

When working with first-generation college students, I noticed they faced a recurring pattern of obstacles and barriers. Our team helped them persist in overcoming these challenges to gain acceptance into higher education. One unforgettable young woman, Berenice, was a remarkable Latina who, despite the loss of her mother, remained steadfast in her pursuit of making a meaningful impact. With aspirations of becoming an attorney, she enrolled in Georgetown University, and after completing law school she sought me out so we could catch up. Her journey taught me a valuable lesson: women of color need mentors who can support and guide them through their academic and professional endeavors. We share a profound understanding of the significance of our collective experiences, and these transcend cultural and language differences. When as women of color we gain knowledge and wisdom from one another, we grow personally and collectively.

While women mentors have been incredibly important in my life, I would be remiss not to acknowledge the invaluable contributions Black men have also made. Throughout my life I have been fortunate to have several male mentors who have had a profound impact on my life. Dr. Terry Flowers, my supervisor at St. Philip's School and Community Center, deserves special recognition. He saw potential in me that I couldn't recognize myself. Dr. Flowers provided me with opportunities that many wouldn't have offered to a thirty-year-old new mom, pushing me to grow and succeed.

Another influential mentor was Greg, a business genius who shared his insights and knowledge with me. My business acumen was limited, but Greg allowed me to observe and learn from his work. He also shared valuable insights that have had a significant impact on my personal and professional growth. Through his social capital, he has opened doors for me in numerous realms.

Throughout my journey God has sent divine helpers who showed up to help me reach my destiny. One happened to be a former White male supervisor who gave me numerous opportunities to thrive. During my PhD studies, Arnie fostered an environment that allowed me to reach my full potential. In a context where it could have been challenging to balance work and academic pursuits, Arnie demonstrated empathy and a genuine willingness to share his knowledge. Recognizing his privilege, Arnie utilized it to create a supportive and inclusive space, enabling me to flourish both personally and professionally.

THE POWER OF MENTORS, COACHES, AND SPONSORS

In order to succeed, it is especially important for women of color to have mentors and sponsors. A mentoring relationship is a crucial part of a support ecosystem. It's based on the experience and knowledge of the mentor and the guidance, support, and advice sought by the individual. Mentors share their expertise to help the individual reach their full potential, improve in a specific area, or achieve their goals. The relationship can be personal or professional.

Data proves that there is power in mentorship in the workplace for promotions and salary increases. In 2006, Sun Microsystems published a study conducted by Gartner and Capital Analytics to evaluate the effects of a company mentoring program.[1] The study found that mentoring had a significant impact on employees' salary grade—25% of those participating in the program experienced a salary grade change compared to 5% of employees not participating. Moreover, the study revealed positive financial benefits for mentors as well. Specifically, 28% of the mentors in the test group had a salary grade change, while only 5% of the mentors in the control group did. These findings highlight the value of mentoring programs in the workplace, demonstrating their ability to benefit both mentors and mentees in terms of career advancement and financial rewards.

While mentorship is critical for upward mobility in the workplace, it unfortunately doesn't happen as often for women of color. The problem is that in the workplace, people tend to mentor those who are most like them. According to Johnson, Thomas, and Brown, most senior-level roles are held by White men, which means their mentors were the same. For women of color, access to mentors is limited or almost nonexistent.[2]

Even when women of color do find someone willing to serve as a mentor, they may or may not be a good fit. When choosing a mentor we often focus on titles and achievements, but these should not be the only criteria. Character is essential. Experience may open doors, but it is character that sustains relationships. A person who lacks integrity is problematic because their true nature behind closed doors may differ from their public persona, making it difficult to trust their truthfulness and consistency.

Jesus' ability to gather and keep twelve men around him for three years has always fascinated me. Their relationship was more than just working, worshiping, and traveling together; they also learned from each other. Jesus had to have been personable and engaging, as nobody would want to spend three years with someone who was not loving, compassionate, and fun-loving. Nobody would want to be constantly reminded of their sins or live in fear of being themselves due to potential condemnation. Jesus' life is a prime example of effective mentorship.

WISDOM WORKS

As women of color in leadership positions, our faith is a lens through which we support others. It is not enough to have a mentor; we must also be willing to impart our wisdom to others. Wisdom, the ability to make sound decisions based on experience, knowledge, and understanding, is of paramount importance in mentoring relationships. It encompasses discerning what is true and valuable, comprehending life's complexities, and applying this understanding in practical and meaningful ways. While often associated with age and experience, wisdom can be cultivated through education, reflection, and introspection. Wisdom empowers individuals to overcome life's obstacles and make meaningful contributions to their communities and the world. *Sophia*, the Greek term for wisdom, connotes a state of sagacity, intelligence, and cleverness. In Proverbs 8:17-23, wisdom is described as a quality that has existed since the beginning of time, underscoring its fundamental significance. Before creation was formed, wisdom existed.

When selecting a mentor, make wisdom your guiding principle. James 3:13 suggests that a wise person is evident through virtuous actions and a humble demeanor. Age alone does not guarantee wisdom; I have encountered many elders who have not gleaned life's lessons. Of course, your objective is not to find perfection, but you do want to identify someone who has derived learning from their experiences. And you're looking for more than just guidance—this is someone you want to emulate.

I notice a lot of people throw the term "mentor" around without establishing time to sit at the feet of that person. I think about how Jesus spent time with God and reflected his Father as a result. If we are going to benefit from our mentors, we must spend quality time with them. I vividly recall Merriam, one of my mentees who demonstrated exceptional time management skills. She scheduled our meetings in advance and prepared an agenda to optimize our time together. Her goal was not merely to receive status updates but to leverage my expertise and tools to accomplish our objectives effectively.

Mentoring others is a crucial aspect of personal and professional growth. In the article "Mentoring While Black & Female: The Gendered Literacy Phenomenon of Black Women Mentors," the authors identified four main themes for Black women mentoring in academia.[3] These themes, which I have modified slightly for relevance beyond academia, can serve as a guide for anyone who mentors others, regardless of field or background:

- Leveraging cultural teachings and lessons
- Navigating challenging and unsafe workplace environments
- Engaging in community service and giving back
- Sustaining and enduring through unspoken understanding and support.

When as women of color we impart our knowledge to others through mentorship, we contribute formidably to our communities. We help establish secure environments for ourselves and each other. What might happen if we were even more deliberate in our development of others?

As a young woman I knew the importance of mentorship, but it wasn't until I was much older that I encountered the term *sponsor*. Many of us confuse these roles, but author Rosalind Chow makes the distinction: mentors provide guidance and advice, while sponsors advocate for their protégés.[4] She suggests that a sponsor is a type of intermediary impression manager, assuming the role of brand manager and publicist for the protégé and shaping how others perceive their potential and worth. It's important to note that the central relationship in sponsorship is not between protégé and sponsor but rather between the sponsor and the audience they aim to influence on behalf of their protégé.

Zeb Strong played a significant role in ensuring my visibility and recognition during college and beyond. He made sure I was included in important discussions and that my perspective was represented even when I wasn't physically present. Zeb was not just a mentor but a sponsor, advocating for me. Thanks to his active support, I had the opportunity to lead a workshop at a conference for minority students. That experience opened doors for me, as I was later invited to speak at Notre Dame.

I firmly believe in the power of sponsorship. I've not only had sponsors such as Zeb but I've played that role for others. I've helped nonprofit leaders secure funding by advocating for them in their absence, and whenever I discover a funder's interests, I approach them with a list of organizations worthy of their consideration.

Within my professional network I am fortunate to have coaches as well as mentors and sponsors. Coaches are not solely cheerleaders; they also serve as guides, offering goal-oriented support that is structured, collaborative, and time-bound (not typically indefinite). Coaches can help with anything from managing a transition to improving health to boosting performance. Sandy is a coach who helped me during a time of significant transition, providing me with a tool that helped me pay attention to my self-talk. There are many different types of coaches available and certifications vary. Find someone who has the expertise and experience necessary to help you reach your goals.

It's important to note that coaches are not therapists, and every leader needs a therapist in their life at some point. A therapist can enhance personal and professional growth, address past traumas, and assist with the challenges of everyday life. We often don't realize that we bring all of who we are to the workplace, and unresolved childhood traumas have an impact on how we show up as leaders.

Leaders cannot lead in isolation. As an entrepreneur I have discovered the importance of surrounding myself with a supportive team. In the early stages of my career, I had mentors who provided guidance and support. As my network expanded, I identified sponsors who could advocate for me and open doors to new opportunities. Throughout my journey, coaches have been consistent sources of wisdom and encouragement. Notably, my mother has been a steadfast coach, listening attentively and offering valuable advice.

Similarly, you deserve a team of individuals who can help you thrive in all aspects of your life. Why not consider forming a personal board of directors consisting of mentors, coaches, and sponsors? You may not need all of these roles at once, but the seasons of your life will determine what you require. For a list of resources that can help you find this kind of support, see the appendix at the end of this book.

My own board of directors developed gradually over time as I recognized the need for diverse perspectives, skills, and visions to support my growth. I would not have gone back to school in my forties to get a PhD without these people affirming that I could do it. My board of directors is not like a typical board. They don't meet to discuss me collectively—thank God! I use this small team individually to provide insight and consensus when I'm making a big decision.

According to Melissa Eisler, a personal board of directors is a group of five to ten individuals who can assist you in making sound decisions, provide advice and feedback, challenge your assumptions, expand your professional network, brainstorm and evaluate ideas, and generally broaden your perspective and thinking. Eisler also believes that your personal board of directors should include not just supporters but also individuals who will challenge your perspectives.[5]

I hold a different view. While it's not necessary to surround oneself solely with individuals who agree with every decision made, an adversary who openly opposes you can create significant challenges, especially for a woman of color. We are already experiencing racism and sexism, and with so few safe spaces, let's not create an environment that's potentially harmful.

The Bible reminds us of the importance of wise counsel (Proverbs 11:14; 12:15; 15:22). There are also many examples of mentorship—David and Jonathan, Elijah and Elisha, Moses and Joshua. Scripture underscores the necessity of mentors, for our faith shapes our beliefs and actions.

The Scripture "Iron sharpens iron; so a man sharpens his friend's countenance" (Proverbs 27:17) emphasizes the significance of individuals in our lives who challenge and inspire us to grow. Mentors play a crucial role in shaping our character and helping us reach our full potential. Similarly, being a mentor to others allows us to share our wisdom and experiences, contributing to their personal and professional development. Through these relationships we sharpen one another and become stronger, wiser, and more capable individuals.

Proverbs 1:5, "that the man of understanding may attain to sound counsel," reminds us that even as leaders we don't possess all the answers. Our success relies on the individuals we surround ourselves with. A wise leader actively listens to gain new knowledge and seeks counsel from those who possess understanding.

In the same way that Jesus assembled the disciples to form the first board of directors, each offering unique gifts and talents to fulfill his mission, it is essential to be intentional in identifying individuals who can assist you in accomplishing your mission. How are you strategically seeking out and recognizing individuals with complementary skills and expertise who can contribute to your goals and aspirations? How are you discipling others personally and professionally?

SCRIPTURES TO CONSIDER

"Go and make disciples of all nations, baptizing them in the name of the Father and of the Son and of the Holy Spirit, teaching them to observe all things that I commanded you. Behold, I am with you always, even to the end of the age." Amen. (Matthew 28:19-20)

One who walks with wise men grows wise,
> but a companion of fools suffers harm. (Proverbs 13:20)

Instruct a wise person, and he will be still wiser.
> Teach a righteous person, and he will increase in learning. (Proverbs 9:9)

QUESTIONS FOR REFLECTION

1. If you have a sponsor, coach, or mentor, are you actively communicating and collaborating with them? If not, what's preventing you from doing so?
2. What process did you use to choose your current advisers? What qualifications and merits led you to select them?
3. If you do not have a mentor, sponsor, or coach, are there individuals who could serve those roles in your life? Write down the names of three to five people to prayerfully consider approaching.

PRAYER

Dear Lord, Jesus was an excellent mentor. He made the effort to comprehend his followers' personalities and was open to guidance from God. This allowed him to gain wisdom that he utilized to support and direct his disciples. Motivate me to be open to mentorship, to learn from others, and to use my knowledge to assist others in developing. In the precious name of Jesus, amen.

PROFILES IN LEADERSHIP

The Ceilings All Around Us: Sarah's Story

Sarah is an Asian female in her midforties working as a pharmacy director. She has extensive experience working with people with HIV/AIDS and those who are low-income, underserved, and underinsured. She has faced many barriers as a woman of color working in health care, particularly those unique to Asian women.

One of the most challenging situations Sarah faces is how others see her. "People see me and assume whatever they will assume, usually a combination of perceived age, gender, and ethnicity," Sarah says. "Not so much from coworkers, as health care is a diverse field among practitioners, although administration is still very White. Yet the challenge is from patients."

Sarah was an immigrant to the United States. She grew up being told that White America would not respect her or let her succeed unless she worked in health care. "There was a perception that health care was more merit-based," she says. "Racism was assumed in America, so I was taught that I had to choose the most merit-based field possible in order to have a chance at success."

Many women of color do not have the freedom to be themselves in the workplace. Like Sarah, they walk a fine line between being "nice" and being a doormat. "People expect me to be nice or else I am not being a team player or am being combative," Sarah says. "This perpetuates the myth of the model minority. I can't 'succeed' if they don't think I'm nice, or I'll get patient complaints if I'm not (what I perceive as) obsequious. And because health care is essentially customer service akin to retail, it really matters what patients think of me. So in this sense, it almost contradicts what I was taught: entry into health care may be more merit-based than other fields, but it's almost like accepting the bamboo ceiling."

Those above Sarah on the corporate ladder are mostly White and male, and they're usually old enough to hold the stereotypes mentioned above.

"They expect a level of 'courtesy' well past professionalism," Sarah says. "If I am just professional, it doesn't seem like enough. It seems that the mostly White male older generation still expects me to fawn."

Sarah points out the toxicity that exists in health care and retail when customers behave poorly and staff must face it with a smile. "I have had patients want me to call them 'sir' or 'mister,' and they get mad because I didn't thank them for being a veteran or 'giving me my freedom,'" she says. "They tell me an Asian person can never understand and call me things like 'China doll.' And I can't address it or say anything back."

Sarah refers to this experience as the Mantle of the White Coat. "It's the idea that being a health care provider is so holy and provides such great service that that alone should feed me; that because I'm fulfilling such a lofty and noble cause, I should be able to turn the other cheek at all times; we are above such things as wanting or needing common courtesy and respect," she says. "It took me a long time to come to grips with this. This isn't specifically a gripe against racism in health care, as even White persons are expected to put up with some bad behavior from patients."

Lessons for Younger Women

- Try to get emotional or professional support from someone who understands being a woman of color. That woman doesn't need to be in the same professional space as you or work with you. She just needs to be encouraging and supporting.
- East Asian women are taught to be deferential and ignore their own thoughts and gut feelings, so we absolutely need someone who encourages us and pushes us in a positive direction. Find someone who pushes you to speak up, to contradict, to say no, to set boundaries.

Dealing with Racism, Sexism, and Other "Isms"

- "A lot of times, older White men see me and assume I'm too young to know anything, cannot understand them, or am not as good as a White counterpart. The racism is mostly from White people, the sexism is mostly from men, and the classism is from both."

- "A couple of times I have played dumb about xenophobia and racism just to point out the situation, and they are very hesitant to elaborate. For example, one man came in wearing a 'Don't Tread on Me' shirt so I played dumb and asked him what that shirt was about. He kind of mumbled and said 'political stuff.' I asked what kind of political stuff and he wouldn't elaborate."

Sarah's journey also highlights the challenges of intergroup dynamics. Oppression doesn't just happen by the dominant culture to those who are marginalized. Often, marginalized people do the same thing to one another.

- "I have experienced a lot of negativity from the gay and trans community. Maybe they learned the behavior—to put down someone so you feel better, or to be super defensive—but they assume because I am an Asian female and possibly young, I am heterosexual or disagree with the gay-trans community. A lot of people in that community have gone out of their way to say passively negative things to me ('Your jacket is really ugly') or say they'd rather see the White pharmacist, to outright negative things ('Why are you even here? I'm sure you hate gays'). I understand their reaction far better than a man wearing a 'Don't Tread on Me' shirt, as the gay-trans community are obviously victims of systemic oppression. So I don't hold it against them as much as I would bad behavior from a White male or a White person in general."

5

Rejection and Trauma in the Workplace

I KNOW FROM PERSONAL EXPERIENCE how powerful rejection can be in the workplace. I applied to numerous positions in 2010, and the number of rejection letters I received was unfathomable. Despite my education and experience, hearing that someone else was a "better fit" made me wonder what I was missing. It became easy to apply for lesser roles to avoid disappointment.

A recent *Forbes* article discusses an important discovery: women tend to avoid applying for high-level executive roles if they were previously rejected for a similar position.[1] This trend stems from long-standing social conventions that assign women assisting functions while linking leadership tasks with men. When women are refused professional chances, it cements the view that they must overcome major obstacles in order to reach upper management roles, especially for women of color.

The tragic passing of Dr. Antoinette "Bonnie" Candia-Bailey, a senior administrator at Lincoln University in Missouri, highlights the mental health struggles women of color face in their careers. Candia-Bailey took her own life on January 8, 2024, after confiding in the university's president, John Mosely, about her severe depression and anxiety. Email communications shared with local media showed that Candia-Bailey had requested leave and accommodation under the Family Medical

Leave Act and Americans with Disabilities Act for her condition. They also revealed a deteriorating relationship between Candia-Bailey and Moseley. When Candia-Bailey complained to the university board about her treatment, they responded that the board was not responsible for personnel issues. Candia-Bailey felt unsupported and believed she was set up to fail, which many women of color experience.

Two other women of color working in high-level academic administration recently passed away as well: Dr. Orinthia Montague, president of Volunteer State Community College, and JoAnne A. Epps, acting president of Temple University.[2] Their sudden deaths sent shockwaves through the community of women of color working in academia. It was widely believed that the demands and pressures that come with these leadership roles contributed significantly to their premature deaths. Author Alexia Hudson-Ward highlights in her blog that BIPOC (Black, Indigenous, and other people of color) women often face trauma and stress in academia and states that they are "battle-weary." They experience being "'presumed incompetent' by some White colleagues and leaders . . . measured against unfair performance expectations, fighting against stereotype threat and, at times, hostility from other people of color within her institution."[3]

In their books *Presumed Incompetent* (2012) and *Presumed Incompetent II* (2020), authors Carmen G. González and Angela P. Harris explore the experiences of female academics who have been deemed unqualified due to stereotypes and biases. These include the belief that women of color attained their positions only because of affirmative action policies and that their research is not as rigorous as that of their White colleagues.[4] Overcoming the need to constantly prove my own worth is a challenge I've faced personally. After experiencing multiple job-related traumas and rejections, I became more selective about the opportunities I pursued. These demanding roles can lead to immense mental, physical, and emotional stress, which can have severe consequences, including death.

BIBLICAL POINT OF VIEW

Many of us can relate to the story of Leah, Jacob, and Rachel in Genesis 29, which explores the experience of being rejected. Jacob, after deceiving his brother Esau and taking his birthright, was forced to leave his family and find refuge with his uncle Laban, who was even more deceitful than Jacob.

In Laban's household lived two daughters, the older Leah, who had weak eyes, and the younger Rachel, who possessed exceptional beauty. Jacob's heart belonged to Rachel, so he made a deal to serve Laban for seven years in order to marry her. Laban agreed. With a love that made the years fly by, Jacob completed his seven years of service for Rachel.

But Laban tricked Jacob into marrying Leah instead. Jacob was infuriated, and he insisted on marrying Rachel as well. So Laban told Jacob he had to work for him seven more years. Jacob readily agreed, because he loved Rachel more than Leah.

It's not hard to envision the emotional agony and hurt Leah likely felt, knowing her husband did not want her and favored her sister instead. The pain of being rejected can profoundly influence our sense of self and life path, molding who we grow to be.

In an unexpected turn of events, the Lord showed favor to Leah, who was disdained by her husband, by blessing her with fertility, while Rachel, her rival, was unable to conceive. Leah named her first son Reuben, expressing her faith that the Lord had seen her affliction and that now her husband would love her. With her second son, Leah believed the Lord understood her distress and named him Simeon. With the birth of her third son, Levi, Leah hoped her husband would finally devote himself to her. In a moment of thankfulness, Leah conceived her fourth son and proclaimed she would praise the Lord. Thus, he was named Judah. After this, Leah was no longer able to have children.

The names of Leah's sons reflect the progression of her emotions. Reuben represented her optimism that giving birth would earn her husband's affection. The arrival of Simeon and later Levi made it clear that her husband's attitude was unmoved. Though faced with this reality, Leah came to recognize God's active role in her life. She gradually accepted her circumstances, and by the time Judah was born, her attention had shifted from seeking her husband's approval to appreciating God's steadfast kindness.

But Leah's anguish again affected how she saw herself. Worried she would not be able to have more children for Jacob, she tried to gain his love and respect in other ways. Even when she was able to get pregnant again—and despite her impassioned explanation of the sacrifices she had made for him—Jacob stayed detached.

Like Leah, many of us strive for appreciation, fairness, and acceptance in our personal lives and careers. Despite our hard work and commitment, our efforts don't seem to pay off and we become discouraged. When we feel we are not treated justly, how can we move past mourning our unmet goals and instead praise God amid our suffering? How can we set limits and prioritize our well-being to prevent overexertion and maintain our health?

EMOTIONAL INTERGENERATIONAL TRAUMA

In life we often don't fully appreciate the long-term impact of traumatic events. Experiences like workplace abuse, sexual misconduct, prejudice, unfair treatment, unhealthy company environments, natural catastrophes, losing loved ones, and difficult childhoods can all be emotionally traumatic. A study by the World Health Organization (WHO) discovered that a worrying 70% of people in twenty-four nations have gone through trauma, experiencing 3.2 traumatic incidents over their lifetime, on average.[5] These traumas profoundly affect our self-image, influencing our identity and how we operate in professional settings.

Trauma, as characterized by the American Psychological Association, is a response to an extremely stressful event that provokes intense emotions and manifests through both psychological and physiological reactions.[6] A relevant example that many identify with is the novel *The Color Purple*, which depicts through fictional characters the experiences of African American women in the early 1900s. The protagonist, Celie, endures separation from her family, abuse, rejection, and sexual and physical violence from people who were supposed to keep her safe. As a result she suffers internalized harm, including insecurity, a belief that women should be beaten for disobedience, and feelings of shame and embarrassment. Notably, each woman in the book goes through some form of mistreatment and ultimately seeks both personal freedom and solidarity with others.[7]

As the novel shows, exclusion and subjugation have tormented generations, and they continue through contemporary problems such as police violence, prejudice, and racism at work. Recognizing this trauma and its impact is necessary on our road to healing. Joy DeGruy calls this phenomenon "post-traumatic slave syndrome," which refers to the cross-generational injury endured by African Americans that began in enslavement in this country. The trauma of family divisions, assaults, beatings, and other horrors combined with historical and current racism and discrimination shapes who we are today. Post-traumatic slave syndrome is similar to post-traumatic stress disorder, involving feelings of hopelessness and isolation and an attitude of self-destruction.[8] Behaviors and psychological patterns include:

- Extreme mistrust and perceived harmful intentions of others
- Aggressive acts toward oneself, one's belongings, and other people—including friends and family members
- Helplessness and feeling unable to change circumstances
- A distorted self-image
- Hostility or strong dislike of others or particular circumstances, including physical features, principles, and customs shared within one's cultural or ethnic community

THE GENERATIONAL IMPACTS OF HISTORICAL TRAUMA

The effects of trauma are passed down through generations. While this section is not comprehensive, it is designed to provide a brief overview of the experience of women of color and to identify similarities in their journeys.

Many common features of the immigrant woman of color's experience lead to generational trauma. Often immigrants of color live in poor urban areas, trying to adapt and survive, and their challenges can be compounded by conservative religious traditions. Historical patterns of marginalization in the surrounding society repeat and reinforce harm. When women of color experience harm or abuse in the workplace today, the impact is often greater because of the legacy of these historical patterns.

A close friend of mine, a successful Asian American professional, often talks about her parents' journey immigrating from Korea to America. Her parents' traumatic experiences left them with unresolved pain that continued into my friend's childhood, which was marked by emotional distance and lack of care. Now that my friend is an adult, she and her parents have a disconnected relationship where neither can fully connect on an emotional level or understand the harm done in the past.

Asian Americans carry the burden of past trauma stemming from imperialism and colonialism. Over the twentieth century and beyond, Asia has seen war, political unrest, and lack of resources, leading to waves of migration to America.[9] These historical traumas and their social, psychological, and political effects have substantially impacted the adaptation, adjustment, mental and physical health, and relationship quality of Asian American families across generations. However, these traumatic experiences are rarely discussed.[10] Asian Americans' access to their ethnic and racial history is constrained by dominant narratives in America that tend to overlook their experiences.[11]

In my home I had the privilege of being exposed to an intimate and moving story. My former husband, who is of mixed Black and Japanese descent, shared his mother's experiences as an Asian woman facing separation from her loved ones in the 1950s. After marrying a Black man, she found herself completely isolated from her relatives until her death over fifty years later. One especially traumatic incident happened when my sister-in-law was a little girl. A stove explosion severely injured her mother's face. Her mother's limited ability to speak English made it hard for her to get help right away, forcing her to depend on her young daughter for assistance. Considering this distressing experience and her subsequent isolation from family, I can only envision the depth of agony she endured throughout her life.

Those who have endured historical trauma often keep their experiences to themselves, even from family members. This silence can put pressure on the relationship between traumatized parents and their children. Parents who don't talk openly about their trauma may continue being affected by it without realizing, which leads their children to guess at the reasons for their actions.[12] Children who don't know their family's background can have trouble forming a unified and affirmative sense of identity.[13]

The suffering of Latina immigrant sisters is often disregarded. The National Women's Law Center points out that Latina immigrant women attempting to flee sexual violence and community conflict are stereotyped as opportunistic—just trying to give birth and find jobs in the United States.[14] Compared to other women of color, Latina immigrant women face a much higher risk of intimate partner violence, increasing their likelihood of post-traumatic stress disorder, long-term health problems, and inequities. Due to a lack of money, many women stay in abusive relationships instead of seeking help. Their children, who need a sense of safety and security, are deeply impacted by these situations.[15] This isn't just an issue Latina women face; many women of color often stay in dangerous relationships because of their need for financial support.

There are many examples of trauma being passed down through generations. A 2015 study found that parental trauma exposure correlates with a higher risk of developing post-traumatic stress disorder, mood disorders, and anxiety disorders in their children.[16] Remarkably, biological alterations associated with stress-related disorders have been observed in the children of trauma survivors, even if those children have not themselves experienced trauma or reported psychiatric disorders. Research suggests that the traumatic experiences faced by Holocaust survivors may have had genetic consequences, potentially influencing the genetic makeup of their offspring.[17]

Many people unknowingly bear the emotional burden of their ancestors' experiences. Daily triggers such as personal experiences and current events can activate these latent traumas. When we arrive at the workplace, we bring with us a wealth of experiences, beliefs, and values that influence our leadership style. Without an understanding of our history, culture, and family lineage, we may unwittingly direct negative emotions toward ourselves and others.

TOXIC LEADERSHIP AND COMPOUNDED TRAUMA

Not only are we dealing with historical trauma, but studies show that women of color face marginalization and trauma in their workplaces as well. Specifically in higher education, research indicates that women of color face more obstacles to professional development and achievement than White women do. Many Black women, particularly those working at mostly White colleges, experience feelings of exclusion, seclusion, and social marginalization. This marginalization often translates into a feeling of invisibility.[18] And it's not just academia where discrimination is present. Women of color encounter similar obstacles in global development, nonprofit management, corporate environments, and many other fields.

Many of us have had the unfortunate experience of working with toxic leaders. These individuals aren't simply incompetent; they display a consistent pattern of harmful behavior. Toxic leaders resort to dysfunctional tactics such as deception, intimidation, coercion, and unfair punishment to achieve their own personal goals. Rather than operating out of a commitment to long-term success, they rely on positional power to compel compliance from their followers.[19] The impacts of harmful leadership in the workplace are immense. Research demonstrates that around 50% of people who experienced disrespectful behavior at work reported substantial time lost to preoccupation with it and its likely consequences. Furthermore, more than 25% of those on the receiving end of discourtesy admitted to decreasing their work commitment.[20]

Toxic leaders induce trauma by belittling, bullying, isolating, and demoralizing employees, and they cultivate work environments characterized by fear, guilt, and shame. I have heard from countless individuals who, as a result of such abuse, started to doubt their own capabilities. But these leaders who create chaos, criticize without offering solutions, and blame others to avoid responsibility are often insecure—the source of their toxic behavior.

INSECURITY IN LEADERSHIP

Insecure leaders tend to employ arrogance and a sense of entitlement to conceal their underlying feelings of inadequacy and their need for affirmation and validation. Many workplaces are filled with insecure leaders whose unresolved trauma causes them to wound those they are meant to steward. King Saul in the Bible is a cautionary example of the consequences of allowing insecurity to cloud judgment.

In 1 Samuel 18, the mood is celebratory as the army returns home victorious after David triumphed over the Philistines in battle. Women from all over Israel have assembled to greet King Saul, their ruler. They sing, dance, and play their tambourines, praising Saul for his success in the fight. But their spirits rise even higher as they shout that David, their courageous champion, has killed even more enemies.

Saul is furious when he hears these words. He does not appreciate the people's praise of David and he worries about his position as king. Instead of cherishing Israel's victory and recognizing God's divine intervention, Saul becomes consumed by insecurity. He allows the opinions of others to overshadow his faith and loses sight of God's plan. Insecurity often leads individuals to diminish the accomplishments of others in an attempt to bolster their own self-worth.

As God's favor on David grows, so does Saul's jealousy. He becomes increasingly resentful, driving a wedge between himself and God. Saul's fear of David also intensifies, leading him to make numerous attempts on David's life, escalating the conflict between them.

Insecurity is a dangerous vice that can have devastating consequences. Saul's preoccupation with David eroded his leadership and diminished his capacity for sound decision-making. He repeatedly failed to heed God's directives, leading to far-reaching ramifications including—ultimately—the loss of the kingdom of Israel. Instead of facing his shortcomings, Saul resorted to making excuses, a coping mechanism that deflected responsibility for his actions.

Unlike Saul, David came to power because of his steadfast faith in God. He cultivated his belief instead of giving in to fear. David showed kindness and empathy, putting the welfare of his people before chasing personal fame. His devotion to God made God call him "a man after my own heart" (Acts 13:22 NIV). David had faith in God's capabilities and recognized his own shortcomings. Although he erred frequently, his obedience to God created an enduring legacy that is still commemorated today.

I have encountered both exceptional and harmful leaders throughout my career. My first job out of graduate school was with a governmental agency. The leader became so threatened by my success that she gave my responsibilities to my administrative assistant. Every day the admin came to me for help while I technically had nothing to do. Everyone knew it was unfair and a punishment. Even executive leaders in the organization remarked to me that they were aware of it and it was wrong. But nothing was done, and I finally quit to launch my business. Sadly, these were women of color.

Fortunately, I also had amazing leaders like Beth and Leonetta, who taught me strategy, grace, and compassion. Their leadership shaped my own style. I view myself as a shepherd, guiding and protecting my team through my stewardship.

The adage "hurt people hurt people" serves as a reminder that unaddressed pain can manifest in our interactions with others. As leaders, our actions and decisions have both immediate and lasting consequences. Thus it is imperative that we consider the impact we have on our team members and the legacy we will leave behind.

REFRAMING LEADERSHIP IN THE WORKPLACE

As a leader, I've found it invaluable to intentionally use the appropriate "lens"—i.e., viewpoint or perspective. Just as an optometrist uses different lenses to assess our vision, our past experiences, particularly traumatic ones, can distort how we see things. Without a structured approach, we may personalize and misinterpret situations. Authors Boleman and Deal have provided guidance by introducing four lenses that can be applied in the workplace to gain a clearer understanding of any given situation.[21]

1. The structural frame emphasizes policies, procedures, and systems.
2. The political frame concentrates on power dynamics, conflict resolution, and coalition formation.
3. The symbolic frame involves an organization's purpose, rituals, and symbols.
4. The human relations frame focuses on interpersonal relationships and the well-being of individuals within an organization.

Throughout my career, I have frequently applied the human relations frame to my workplace assessments. However, I have also recognized the limitations of this approach, as there are often other factors at play. Sometimes I have wrongly concluded that people disliked me when, in reality, it was my own personal pain speaking rather than a reflection of the situation. These frames are influenced by our experiences, which can include the trauma of racism, sexism, and classism, among others.

ADDRESSING TRAUMA AS LEADERS

As leaders we must be mindful not to let our internalized pain affect others. Many of us have endured difficult experiences, both personal and professional, at the hands of others. Often we suffer in silence and do not address these issues. But our decision to remain silent can affect those we interact with. Leah's story in the Bible illustrates how rejection and other traumatic experiences can shape our perceptions of ourselves and others. It's important to consider how people will remember you and your leadership. How do they perceive your behavior and interactions with them?

In Hebrews 13:7, believers are encouraged to reflect on the lives of their leaders who have imparted the word of God. By contemplating the results of our leaders' lifestyles, we can find inspiration and imitate the unwavering faith demonstrated by these individuals.

If imitation is the sincerest form of flattery, will others be inspired to emulate your approach to life, faith, and action? Or will they see a tendency to view individuals as inferior or deserving of pity, mere means of boosting your self-esteem while you avoid opportunities for personal growth and refuse to learn from those who challenge or intimidate you?

As believers, our leadership choices hold great significance. While we readily criticize world leaders, we too often overlook the troubling actions of leaders within our own communities of faith. Biblical examples, such as the family dynamics of Leah, Jacob, Rachel, and their servants, as well as the destructive reign of Saul, illustrate how unresolved trauma, toxic leadership, and misguided perspectives can have devastating consequences for individuals, organizations, and communities.

SCRIPTURES TO CONSIDER

Coming to him, a living stone, rejected indeed by men, but chosen by God, precious. (1 Peter 2:4)

Then you will say in your heart, "Who has conceived these for me, since I have been bereaved of my children
and am alone, an exile, and wandering back and forth?
Who has brought these up?
Behold, I was left alone. Where were these?"

The Lord Yahweh says, "Behold, I will lift up my hand to
the nations,
and lift up my banner to the peoples.
They shall bring your sons in their bosom,
and your daughters shall be carried on their shoulders.
Kings shall be your foster fathers,
and their queens your nursing mothers.
They will bow down to you with their faces to the earth,
and lick the dust of your feet.
Then you will know that I am Yahweh;
and those who wait for me shall not be disappointed."
(Isaiah 49:21-23)

Whoever listens to you listens to me, and whoever rejects you rejects me. Whoever rejects me rejects him who sent me. (Luke 10:16)

QUESTIONS FOR REFLECTION

1. What are your trauma-related triggers?
2. How do these triggers show up in your personal life? Professional life?
3. How are you addressing your trauma?

PRAYER

Heavenly Father, I come before you with a humble heart to seek your healing power through the Holy Spirit. I believe that you, as my eternal Father, will never reject or abandon me. I find acceptance, love, value, and support through your Son, Jesus. Thank you for embracing me unconditionally, regardless of my imperfections. I ask that you speak to my heart through your Word, reminding me of your profound love and care. Reassure me that you will never forsake me and that I can always trust in your presence.

May your Word renew my mind and break the root of rejection that has manifested in my life as anger, bitterness, perfectionism, and despair. Through the blood of Jesus, I declare freedom from these negative emotions. In Jesus' name, amen.[22]

PROFILES IN LEADERSHIP

Delays Are Not Denials: Katelyn's Story

Katelyn is a Black woman in her late forties who is an entrepreneur providing consulting for organizations. For more than thirty years she's been in roles spanning academia, local government, and nonprofit management. Katelyn's journey has been plagued with disparities as a result of her race and age.

She's been targeted and harassed in the workplace, even being verbally abused in a meeting, which led to her resignation. Race has not been the only challenge she's experienced in the workplace. She has been bypassed for opportunities because she would not engage in behaviors that could be perceived as compliance with sexual harassment. She's witnessed young women being given opportunities potentially as a result of their appearance or their willingness to comply.

But these delays were not denials. They became the setup for her success. The support of elders in the Black community created pivotal opportunities that altered Katelyn's career trajectory. Throughout her career, she received significant support and mentorship from older White men and Black community leaders.

Katelyn has faced discrimination in the workplace because of her size, geographic origin, speech pace, and youth. Her greatest challenges have arisen in interactions with other Black women who saw her as competition or a threat. Yet these did not deter her from pursuing her dream of making an impact in the community or partnering with Black women.

An avid reader and learner, Katelyn is heavily influenced by team concepts from mentors in military and intelligence. Katelyn emphasizes that training and development, teamwork, and not asking team members to do anything she wouldn't do herself as the formula for successful leadership.

Katelyn grew up in a diverse environment and faith did not play a significant role in her workplaces until she moved to the South, where religion was used divisively in her work environments.

Lessons for Younger Women

- Take personal accountability and seek safe spaces.
- Don't doubt your feelings and what you experience: Document incidents and utilize HR departments to ensure issues are on record.

Dealing with Racism, Sexism, and Other "Isms"

- Sometimes directness and adherence to policy and process are misconstrued as being difficult or noncollaborative.
- Challenges in being the youngest, the only, or the first in various environments lead to the need to prove competence continually. Stop feeling the need to prove yourself.

6

Intersectionality and Leadership

WHEN I WAS GROWING UP, I remember my mother saying she identified more with being a woman than with being Black. I always saw my Blackness first. Most of the issues I faced in my early career were related more to age and race than gender. As I've gotten older, I value all of my identities and the perceptions attached to each. I am aware of how I express those identities and also how others respond to them. All of us have multiple identities that shape who we are, and I often feel we are forced to choose instead of embracing these various elements of our being. Intersectionality is something all women of color experience.

Kimberlé Crenshaw, a legal scholar, coined the term *intersectionality* to describe how different forms of inequality compound one another. As Crenshaw explains, we tend to view race inequality and gender inequality as separate rather than interconnected issues.[1] However, some individuals face multiple forms of inequality simultaneously, and the total impact is greater than the sum of the parts. As leaders, we must be cognizant of the power and privilege attached to our own identities and those of the people we work with. I personally identify as a Black cisgender woman with a PhD who is Christian and from the Deep South. Examining the interplay between these identities provides insight into each of our experiences with privilege and marginalization.

I am often struck by Kamala Harris as a contemporary example of a woman understanding her power. With an Indian mother and a Black father, Harris grew up around intellectuals and activists in Oakland and Berkeley. She attended both Howard University, a historically Black university where she pledged Alpha Kappa Alpha sorority, then attended and graduated from the University of Southern California for law school. Harris is a woman who has embraced her power along with her multiple identities, despite being labeled a "DEI candidate" for president of the United States. In the face of being questioned about her background, she demonstrates that for women of color, our difference is our superpower.

I often wonder how things might have been different if biblical women such as Sarah and Hagar understood their own value and worth. Even in a society that does not appreciate women, knowing your inherent value should transform how you see your own life story. Knowing this would change how you perceive yourself and other women around you.

HAGAR'S STRUGGLE

Hagar, Sarah's maidservant from Egypt, was given to Abraham by Sarah when Sarah could not have a child of her own. During her pregnancy, Hagar was mistreated by Sarah. After giving birth to a son, Hagar was sent away into the desert alone. However, even in this difficult transition that was out of her control, God looked after and blessed Hagar.

In the book *Reimagining Hagar*, the author discusses Hagar's various identities.[2] She was a woman. She was Egyptian, an African living among Hebrews. Hagar was a servant given to a man in a nonconsensual arrangement—by today's standards this would be considered rape. She also suffered psychological and emotional abuse. As a result of her situation, Hagar had a child. She did not have a choice in this matter.

The Code of Hammurabi, a set of ancient Babylonian laws, provides insight into the status of women at that time. It held that if a married priestess was childless, her husband could take a second wife, but she could give him a slave to prevent this.[3] When this scenario played out in Abraham's household and Hagar became pregnant, Sarah mistreated her, likely out of jealousy, and blamed Abraham for Hagar's pregnancy. But Abraham avoided responsibility and accountability. While the Code of Hammurabi helps explain why Hagar was mistreated by Abraham and Sarah, let's also remember that Abraham had a covenant with God (Genesis 15:8-20; 17:1-8; 26:5) and was not under these statutes.

Hagar did not accept Sarah's cruel treatment. She fled from the place that had been her residence, abandoning not just the abuse but also the provision of food and lodging. It must have been distressing to be with child and alone. She wound up in the barren region of Shur, a desert east of the Gulf of Suez. The word *shur* means "barrier" and is characterized in Genesis 25:18 as being opposite Egypt on the route to Assyria. In this frightening and unfamiliar land Hagar came across God.

The angel of the Lord found Hagar and instructed her to return to Sarah, as she would give birth to a wild and defiant son. He told her the child would be quarrelsome and contentious. Hagar was the first to name God, calling him *El Roi*, meaning "the God who sees me."

Hagar returned to Sarah and Abraham and delivered Ishmael. Thirteen years later, Sarah gave birth to Isaac, the son of God's covenant with Abraham. Sarah demanded that Hagar and Ishmael be sent away, as she did not want Isaac's inheritance to be shared with Ishmael (Genesis 21:10). With scant regard for their value and personhood, Abraham sent Hagar and Ishmael away: "Abraham rose up early in the morning, and took bread and a container of water, and gave it to Hagar, putting it on her shoulder; and gave her the child, and sent her away. She departed, and wandered in the wilderness of Beersheba" (Genesis 21:14).

Hagar must have been terrified wondering about the fate of her son. When the water ran out, she stepped away in tears, fearing having to watch her son die. Yet again, God saw her even when others did not: "God heard the voice of the boy. The angel of God called to Hagar out of the sky, and said to her, 'What troubles you, Hagar? Don't be afraid. For God has heard the voice of the boy where he is'" (Genesis 21:17). God told her Ishmael would be responsible for a great nation, and her eyes were opened to see a well of water. The Bible states that God was with Ishmael, who was skilled with a bow, and ultimately his mother found him an Egyptian wife. Ishmael had twelve sons, like Jacob, making Hagar the mother of a great nation (Genesis 25:12-15).

In Islam, the story of Hagar and Ishmael differs from other accounts. Muslims believe that Hagar, also known as Hajar, was the daughter of the Egyptian king, who gave her to Abraham's wife Sarah as a gift.[4] Hagar was royalty in one culture and enslaved in another. Juggling these experiences is not uncommon for a woman of color, who must understand that despite oppressive conditions, as believers we are indeed royalty (1 Peter 2:9).

UNDERSTANDING THE POWER OF IDENTITY

Hagar's narrative illuminates several things for us. One is that our personal story can be recounted differently based on viewpoint. As leaders, we must be cognizant of our own story, because our account affects how we perceive ourselves and others. What tale do you relay about yourself? If others were asked about your leadership, how would they describe you? Our identities are linked to the stories we tell: "Narrative identity is the internal and developing account of the self that an individual constructs to find purpose and meaning from their life."[5] Every day we make sense of our circumstances and ourselves.

According to psychologist and educator Beverly Daniel Tatum, identity is a multifaceted concept influenced by many factors, including individual traits, family relationships, historical events, and social and political environments.[6] Our identities are also shaped by the social groups we belong to, such as generation, gender, race, economic class, and religion. Some aspects of identity are assigned to us; some we choose for ourselves, and our core qualities define who we are as individuals.

Intersectionality reminds us that some people have identities that society marginalizes, while others have identities associated with power and privilege. Many people of color, as well as people who are LGBTQIA+, poor, or disabled, experience discrimination, health inequities, economic instability, mental health challenges, and social exclusion. At the same time, having certain privileges such as a PhD or being Christian in the United States can offer advantages and access. We should avoid putting people into simplistic categories without taking the time to understand them as individuals and how their identities are impacted by societal narratives.

It's also important that we embrace our own stories and identities. Our personal narratives have power because they express who we are. When leaders make space to truly listen to and learn from others, it can lead to growth. So can incorporating regular reflection on our past and present experiences into our routines as leaders. Identities are complex, and we should avoid assumptions. Listening to others' stories with openness can lead to positive change.

Hagar's identity is that of a mistreated young woman, voiceless to change her circumstances. She was a woman of color, labeled a slave by one group and a princess by another. She was a mother and someone's daughter. She also knew God and established a legacy through her son Ishmael. She was taken from her family and lived in a time when women had no value.

Hagar's story helps us understand how we may find ourselves in environments unsuited for us. Whether it's a job that underpays or repeatedly passes us over for promotion, we can remember that Hagar stood up for herself by leaving the abuse. Often we can't walk away, but how can we find our voice and prioritize self-care in spaces not designed with us in mind?

Hagar shows us that transition is temporary. From princess to slave to mother of a major world religion, we don't stay where we start. Even if our beginnings involve trauma, pain, abuse, and neglect, with God's help we can still move into our destiny. Hagar understood that God saw her, and God sees each of us. We are never alone.

If Hagar had understood the concept of *ezer kenegdo* from Scripture and what it truly means to be a woman—a warrior and powerful complement—how might her life have been different? This description needs to become part of our self-image as women in the church. Embracing this identity completely transforms how we view ourselves and our life narrative.

Our leadership must be grounded in spiritual completeness and our relationship with God. Even when the world views us negatively and pushes us to the margins of society, we must stand firm in the truth of how God sees us and who God says we are. Our multiple identities should be places of affirmation and empowerment. We should view our intersectional identity as strength and opportunity.

ACTIVITY

One of the most profound experiences I've had is writing a reflective leadership essay. I would encourage you to do the same to reveal the ways in which your leadership journey has shaped who you are. Tell the story of your life, focusing on the role leaders played in shaping who you are. Starting from your childhood, reflect on the leaders, both positive and negative, who influenced you as a teen, young adult, and now. How have these leaders' words and actions molded you into who you are today? What key lessons about leadership have you taken from these experiences? Record your insights on the impact of leadership throughout the different stages of your life.

SCRIPTURES TO CONSIDER

> But as many as received him, to them he gave the right to become God's children, to those who believe in his name. (John 1:12)

> But you are a chosen race, a royal priesthood, a holy nation, a people for God's own possession, that you may proclaim the excellence of him who called you out of darkness into his marvelous light. (1 Peter 2:9)

God created man in his own image. In God's image he created him; male and female he created them. (Genesis 1:27)

QUESTIONS FOR REFLECTION

1. As leaders, how can we ensure that we are focusing our sense of self and purpose in Christ?
2. How can we make sure we are leading from a place of wholeness rooted in our faith? Even in a world that marginalizes us based on some of our characteristics, how do we stand in the truth of who God says we are?
3. How can we as leaders ensure that we are not excluding or isolating others because of their differences or similarities?

PRAYER

Thank you, God, for watching over and understanding me, for watching over and understanding us. Help us to find our true selves in you and see your splendor in other people. Help us to be leaders who acknowledge the might of womanhood and the might within each of us. In the name of Jesus, amen.

PROFILES IN LEADERSHIP

Grace Under Fire: Tamara's Story

Tamara is an example of intersectionality at work. I think many of us can identify with Tamara's journey of not being accepted because of identities that cause us to be marginalized.

Tamara is a Latina woman in her late fifties and an entrepreneur who's been fortunate to have leaders in various careers who cared about performance. For a number of years she's worked for a well-known company where she was promoted consistently. It wasn't that racism didn't exist, but Tamara chose not to make it a focus. "It doesn't mean I have never experienced racism or prejudice, but I've never felt like or 'identified' as a woman of color, even though I am," she says. "I have always believed my performance spoke for itself."

Many women experience harassment or are overlooked for promotions, but this wasn't the case for Tamara. "The most challenging situation was going to work in the same office with my ex-spouse and his new girlfriend," she says. "You could feel the tension in the office every time he and I were on the same shift or in the same vicinity."

For the first time she experienced anxiety. "I felt like I was under a microscope," she says. In order to deal with the pressure, she made it a priority to protect her mental health: "I asked for the time off when I needed it and handled it with as much grace as possible. I knew everyone was anticipating or perhaps wanting drama to unfold, but I was graceful through it all."

Tamara feels that she hasn't been taken seriously as a woman of color. She's experienced rejection from her community because she doesn't speak Spanish well, she's a part of the LGBTQ community, and some political alliances have made acceptance a problem. "I am not invited to participate in some of the group activities," she says.

Tamara's faith is her guiding force in all that she does. Her faith has shaped her views in and outside of the workplace. "I perform for an audience of *one*," she says. "I do my best every single day so I can lay my head on my pillow in peace and gratitude."

Lessons for Younger Women

Make sure you go and stay where you are supported and celebrated! Don't settle or shrink from who you are to make others comfortable. It's the only way we can all grow together.

Dealing with Racism, Sexism, and Other "Isms"

Speak up. Do not tolerate it. "I will also try to educate someone if I sense it was done without malice and purely due to ignorance," Tamara says. "I truly believe all the 'isms' we have created can be undone. There are more good people of all backgrounds than those who purposely try to continue to divide us."

7

Networking and Social Capital

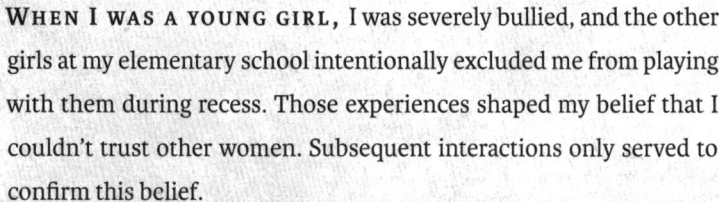

WHEN I WAS A YOUNG GIRL, I was severely bullied, and the other girls at my elementary school intentionally excluded me from playing with them during recess. Those experiences shaped my belief that I couldn't trust other women. Subsequent interactions only served to confirm this belief.

It wasn't until I changed my thinking about relationships with women that I began to attract a wonderful group of female friends into my life. I had to not only alter my perspective on other women but also my self-perception as a woman. When I made this mental shift, my relationships flourished and I unintentionally became dedicated to cultivating meaningful personal and professional connections.

At the time I didn't fully grasp what I was doing, but later in life I realized the importance of building a network. While working on my PhD, I became fascinated with the concept of "social capital," which refers to the value derived from networks, associations, and relationships. Just as money and education are forms of capital that can lead to various accomplishments, relationships can either provide opportunities or limit them. Research by Moore found that factors like education, income, and employment are linked to the size of one's network.[1] One's employment status also determined the composition of their network. Building social capital is essential for advancement.

BUILDING SOCIAL CAPITAL

Social capital can be described a number of ways. One is as a resource composed of social commitments (relationships) that can be converted, under certain circumstances, into economic capital.[2] Putnam, Leonardi, and Nanetti provide this definition: "Social capital encompasses trust, norms, and networks of a social organization, and promotes the efficiency of society by facilitating coordinated actions."[3] Social capital is engagement between individuals or networks that typically generates some kind of benefit in the form of knowledge, association, or financial reward. In simple terms, our connections make things happen.

Problems can arise if we don't understand how to build even basic relationships to excel both personally and professionally. People without social capital are at a disadvantage, especially in a society that relies so much on human interaction, whether face-to-face or through technology. It's critical to understand the impact of social capital on the strength of our organizations. Social capital lets us facilitate transactions through relationships, and it empowers us to advocate for the growth and well-being of our organizations. The pandemic was dangerous not only to our physical health but our social health. The language of "social distancing" was detrimental. We still needed interaction. We still needed relationships. We are social beings.

We must be careful not to view relationships as merely transactional or necessary for monetary gain alone. Social connections are frequently leveraged for profit in today's society. Networking events in cities across America are intended to link people with others who can assist their business pursuits. But these gatherings tend to be homogeneous and exclusive, shutting out those from differing socioeconomic strata, histories, and ethnicities. Without access to insights and connections, it can be tough to thrive financially. A scarcity of knowledge gained through relationships can also restrict organizations' capacity to profit from unique and varied viewpoints.

BONDING AND BRIDGING SOCIAL CAPITAL

There are two kinds of social capital: bonding and bridging. Bonding involves building relationships with others who are similar to oneself. Most individuals find it easy to connect with those who share commonalities, which is an essential human process. Bonding happens between individuals as well as groups that are alike.

While bonding involves connecting with people who are similar to us in terms of background, education, and socioeconomic status, bridging refers to connecting with those who are different from us.[4] Building relationships outside our familiar networks through bridging is important because it helps us obtain useful information that benefits both heterogeneous and homogeneous groups. The problem with staying in homogeneous relationships is that it limits the flow of information to different networks. We should all aim to be bridges between diverse networks and share information across them. An important concern is how we can ensure that we have diverse social circles and disseminate that information to others.

When I was young I observed social capital in action, even though I didn't understand it at the time. I spent summer vacations with my aunt and uncle, who were part of a weekly bowling league. They would inform people about job opportunities or invite individuals to attend church with them. This sharing of information was social capital at work. Many of us restrict our networks because we do not deliberately join groups in our communities. Are you a member of any professional associations or community organizations? I often advise women to serve on the boards of nonprofit groups. It's not just a way to give back but also a chance to expand your network and gain new viewpoints.

As women of color, we tend to operate in collective spaces. Our heritages focus on the group instead of our individual interests. Yet our life experiences can confine us to familiar, safe social circles. We often gravitate toward those who comprehend the difficulties of discrimination, racism, and classism. This comfort zone spares us the hurt of feeling different or rejected by others. But we miss the chance to interact with diverse people if we don't make an effort to broaden our social networks. Even within our own communities, there is diversity. How might we connect with those of differing political views to expand our perspectives?

Many women of color have faced exclusion from professional networks, hampering our career advancement. "Good ole boy" networks are exclusionary circles that have harmed many of us. But we must be careful not to replicate this dynamic within our own networks. I've heard from women of color who were reluctant to refer people of their same race to hiring managers, fearing a bad referral would further marginalize them. Concerns about job security and not wanting to jeopardize one's own position often drive this hesitancy to share contacts, which can restrict opportunities for others. Workplace barriers won't change until we help create that change. I remember HR managers claiming they couldn't find qualified people of color, which irritated me because they weren't looking hard enough. There are many professional organizations and affinity groups for people of color that HR departments should connect with. It's important we join these groups and connect others to these resources.

Networks dominated by men can be difficult for women, especially women of color, to penetrate. Burt's 1998 research revealed that women with more hierarchical networks (or who borrow others' connections) get promotions sooner.[5] Burt's work highlights that women can lag behind in corporations while they're building their networks in order to attain insider versus outsider status. Burt's findings confirm the challenges women face in leadership: building relationships is crucial for advancement.

Although my friends think of me as a master connector, I exhibit both introvert as well as extrovert characteristics. As a child I was painfully shy, and that still comes out at times. Most people experience me as an extrovert, which was something I had to become to avoid being bullied when I was young. As I got older, I became more comfortable coming out of my shell. We ambiverts love people, but we also need space to decompress, because we often take on the energies of others. People who don't know me well can be confused by this. There are times I just need time away—as my daughter says, it's to "recharge my social battery."

For introverts, being around people and networking can be challenging. It's important for introverts to be aware of their boundaries. Instead of going to a networking event, join a club so you are not on the spot to talk until you become comfortable with the environment. You can also set up one-on-one meetings if being in a large group isn't your style. When we are uncomfortable, it's easy to start scrolling on our phones as a distraction—but don't. It's okay to listen more and talk less.

I often advise young women who are building their networks that character matters most. Who you bring with you determines how far you'll go. Relationships thrive on trust and willingness to collaborate. Where there's jealousy, gossip, slander, or hatred, there's division and discord. What's more, not everyone can be in your inner circle. Even Jesus with his twelve disciples had an inner circle of just three. Not everyone can be your confidant.

BIBLICAL POINT OF VIEW

In Numbers 13, Joshua and Caleb were among the twelve spies sent by Moses to scout out the land of Canaan in order to determine whether the Israelites could conquer it.

> Caleb stilled the people before Moses, and said, "Let's go up at once, and possess it; for we are well able to overcome it!"
>
> But the men who went up with him said, "We aren't able to go up against the people; for they are stronger than we." They brought up an evil report of the land which they had spied out to the children of Israel, saying, "The land, through which we have gone to spy it out, is a land that eats up its inhabitants; and all the people who we saw in it are men of great stature. There we

saw the Nephilim, the sons of Anak, who come from the Nephilim. We were in our own sight as grasshoppers, and so we were in their sight." (Numbers 13:30-33)

Caleb and Joshua were the only two in the group who thought it feasible to achieve their goal. These men all shared daily life together, yet Caleb and Joshua had a different perspective. The others didn't just spread false information within the group to raise doubts; they also lacked self-confidence. Most importantly, they relied on their own abilities rather than trusting in God. As a result, Caleb and Joshua were the only ones allowed to enter the Promised Land.

Are you building your network with people who see the vision or those who limit your possibilities because their view is limited? The wrong people in your life can delay your destiny. How can you identify individuals who don't just compliment you but stretch you to become the best version of yourself?

SPONSORS, MENTORS, AND COACHES

I'm often reminded of the contrast between eagles and chickens—one soars high above while the other pecks at the ground. To take flight yourself, you need supportive people to lift you up. Sponsors, mentors, and coaches who can empower you may not resemble you. In high school, a teacher (who happened to be White) took interest in developing my leadership abilities. She championed and encouraged me to run for student government. By my senior year, thanks to her, I became student body secretary. I'll always appreciate this woman for her advocacy. Many others of various backgrounds have also helped me progress. Don't limit possibilities because of differences. We all require collaborators—people who will promote us privately and publicly.

We also need people in the workplace who do not have the same identities we do. People of color may be in the minority in our workplace, and advocates who serve as mentors and open doors can be instrumental in our growth. Research shows that sponsorship especially helps Black women access important training, networking, and advancement opportunities.[6] While mentoring can be valuable, sponsorship is necessary. As women of color, we need personal networks that include advisers, coaches, mentors, and sponsors.

The Bible emphasizes that wisdom is valuable and we should seek the wisdom of others to guide us. As Proverbs 4:7 states, " Wisdom is the principal thing; therefore get wisdom: and with all thy getting get understanding" (KJV). To succeed professionally, we need to use discernment to find people who can assist us. Proverbs 13:10 notes that "only by pride cometh contention: but with the well advised is wisdom" (KJV). We should make every effort to gain wisdom, beginning by identifying wise individuals who can help us thrive and progress in our careers.

OPPORTUNITIES TO BUILD SOCIAL CAPITAL

My friends call me a connector. Relationships are important to me because they make things happen. People who focus on money don't always recognize that money is connected to people. No resource exists without a connection to an individual or a group. June Holley, an amazing mentor, has been instrumental in expanding my view of network weaving. She has especially influenced my commitment to use my network to help others. For every problem I witness, I see a relationship as the solution.

Connectors understand the power of relationships. I make it a point to stay in touch with important people in my life as much as I can. It can be hard when I'm hyper-focused on writing a book or some other time-consuming task, but sending text messages periodically to show love and concern is something simple that helps water the relationship. I know I hate when people show up only when they need something.

Don't make the mistake of seeing only what people can do for you or what you can get out of them. Lead with the type of reputation you want. If you want to be viewed as a person of character and integrity, that has to be expressed in what you do. This extends to your relationships. You can be in community with those who have different values, but spaces that require depth of interaction require a deeper level of connection and synergy. Not everyone can ride with you as you travel to your date with destiny.

Something I strongly encourage women who are building their networks to do is to join a board of directors for a nonprofit organization. In addition to building the capacity of an organization and making a difference through serving others, you meet some amazing people. My network has increased significantly because of volunteering through board service.

Reciprocity is essential. In our world, people throw around the golden rule loosely, but it's not a part of our daily walk. Treat people the way you want to be treated. Want more love in your life? Love on others even more. Want more friends? Be friendly. Keep in mind that you get more of what you put out to others. In doing these things, prepare to watch your network explode with goodness.

ACTIVITY

1. Often relationships must be built intentionally because they don't always happen organically. Make a thirty-, sixty-, and ninety-day strategy to develop your connections. Are there chances monthly to meet someone new for coffee or lunch? Can you utilize LinkedIn and websites like MeetUp.com to join groups and connect with new individuals? If you can't meet in person, how might you explore virtual relationships?

2. When you receive a business card, how soon are you following up? Make a point not to wait until you need someone, but make relationship building and maintenance a part of your routine.

SCRIPTURES TO CONSIDER

A man of many companions may be ruined,
> but there is a friend who sticks closer than a brother.
>> (Proverbs 18:24)

> Don't befriend a hot-tempered man,
>> and don't associate with one who harbors anger:
> lest you learn his ways,
>> and ensnare your soul. (Proverbs 22:24-25)

> A new commandment I give to you, that you love one another. Just as I have loved you, you also love one another. By this everyone will know that you are my disciples, if you have love for one another. (John 13:34-35)

QUESTIONS FOR REFLECTION

1. Do you view yourself as a grasshopper, lacking confidence or feeling inadequate? How might this outlook affect your ability to form connections with others?
2. Who are the individuals who can assist you in achieving success? Do the connections you have represent a range of backgrounds and perspectives?
3. Make a list of these individuals and explain how each one helps you thrive.
4. Are you missing the promises of God because of who is in your camp? Are there individuals you need to leave behind or limit access to your life?

PRAYER

Lord, guide me to cultivate healthy connections in my work and personal spheres that are pleasing to you. Grant me the insight and good judgment to identify worthwhile pursuits and people. You exemplify genuine companionship by sacrificing yourself for us. In my interactions, help me to be dependable, truthful, and present. Allow my integrity to speak louder than my speech so others may see your reflection in me. Bestow upon me the discernment and prudence to choose the right individuals who will aid me in achieving my purpose. In Jesus' name, amen.

PROFILES IN LEADERSHIP

The Power of Sponsorship: Jocelyn's Story

Jocelyn, an African American woman in her thirties or forties, is the first in her family to graduate from college and to hold a corporate job. "I believe this title plays a significant role in my career journey," she says. "I have been in the professional services industry for over fifteen years, working at the same global firm for twelve of those years. Fortunately, I was promoted three times during my tenure to newly created roles. The woman who granted me my first manager position over a decade ago is another woman of color—an Asian woman who took me under her wing. She spoke my name in rooms I was not in!"

Jocelyn was told early in her career to participate in social opportunities so she could build her network. "During an informal gathering outside of work, a member of the executive team made a racial comment toward me in front of a group in a supposedly joking manner," Jocelyn says. "I felt paralyzed and was deeply embarrassed. I was the only woman of color present. I confided in a colleague, who advised me to report the incident to HR. When I approached HR about the issue, they dismissed my concerns and suggested I move on from the incident. Unfortunately, this experience taught me that workplaces sometimes operate in ways that are unfair and unjust."

As a woman of color in an industry where she is underrepresented, Joceyln has been deliberate in forming a community of people who can help each other in their career journeys. "I am proud to say that I have found them, and we have real conversations where we share insights along with the unspoken rules no one tells you," she says.

Many women of color are concerned about being stereotyped as difficult or as being complainers. Jocelyn knows this too well: "One of the key challenges I encounter as a leader is a scarcity or inefficient use of resources, an issue I've communicated within the organization. What distinguishes me as a leader from some of my colleagues of diverse backgrounds is my commitment to persevering and achieving results without resorting to complaints or publicizing issues. I tend to hold it in and 'make it work.'"

Jocelyn spent twelve years at one global firm and decided to leave to advance her career: "It was a tough decision in some ways and I was nervous. I had never negotiated a salary (I was just 'happy to be there' and have a corporate job in a building downtown with free parking... I know, I know!), and I was out of the loop on pay since I'd worked at the same organization for so long."

Jocelyn researched average pay bands but knew to call up another woman of color in the same industry. "She graciously offered to lay out her entire career journey, highlighting every time she moved firms and what her salary was for each move," Jocelyn says. "Additionally, I had the opportunity to hear from the previous position owner, who I knew, and he told me his salary. Going into negotiations, all of this intel armed me with the ability to know what I should be asking for. I am forever grateful for that because we all know the stats of how much less women of color make compared to White males. Conversations like these, I believe, help move the mark."

Joceyln's faith has been an essential part of her career journey. "My faith has helped me believe that what is for me is for me," she says. "For example, I've interviewed for positions I knew I was qualified for but did not get. It's also easy to look around and see others you feel don't deserve a certain role or you ask yourself, 'How did they get there?' I know I have. Although I may not see it at the time or understand it, I have trust in God and believe there's a reason he doesn't want me there and that he has something bigger and better for me."

Lessons for Younger Women

- Develop your expertise, show your value, and foster true relationships: "I learned the hard way that working hard with your head down will not get you promoted," Jocelyn says. "At the beginning of my career, I was 'just happy to be here.' Now I know the value I bring."

- Find allies at work who can advocate for you. The higher you go up, the more political it is. Find your community outside your workplace. Remember your value (you are unique). Know what you can and cannot take and walk away, if needed. Take care of your mental health and find a good therapist.

Dealing with Racism, Sexism, and Other "Isms"

Joceyln recognizes the power of allies and advocates in her journey. "Highly educated and well-paid individuals are my internal clients, and I am in a client service-oriented role," Jocelyn says. "Some managing partners have restricted my access to partner meetings because I'm not one, while others, like my current local managing partner, recognize the importance of my presence and see me as the strategist I am. He understands that in order for me to perform my job to the highest standards, I need a seat at the table. Fortunately, he has extended a standing invitation to me."

8

Emotional and Spiritual Intelligence as a Strategy

WHEN A FORMER BOSS QUIT, I was panicked because she was one of the few leaders I'd had who exhibited a keen ability to read the room and understand what was being said. She reminded me of what leadership theorist and author Ronald Heifeitz says: that leaders must listen to the words beneath the song. She had an ability to understand what was going on even if it was not stated. The next supervisor did not have this ability, and it caused challenges for the organization. People left in droves because of the leader's inability to understand what was going on beyond written reports.

Emotional intelligence is crucial for achieving leadership success. It enables us to truly connect with our teams. Without emotional intelligence, we may overlook many unspoken cues. As defined by Mental Health America, emotional intelligence refers both to comprehending your own emotions and to understanding those of others.[1] There are five main components of emotional intelligence: self-awareness (recognizing your emotions), self-regulation (managing your emotions), motivation (using emotions to achieve goals), empathy (understanding others' emotions), and social skills (building relationships through emotional awareness). Individuals with high emotional intelligence can identify their feelings, grasp what those feelings signify, and comprehend how their emotions affect their actions and other people.

Best-selling author Daniel Goleman argues that by teaching people to attune to their emotions intelligently and expand their compassion for others, organizations can transform from within to create positive change.[2] Goleman's framework categorizes emotional competencies into personal competencies, such as self-awareness and self-management, and social competencies, such as social awareness and relationship management. Effective leaders recognize the importance of emotional intelligence for team performance and collaboration.

BUILDING OUR EMOTIONAL VOCABULARY

Too many of us only understand being happy, sad, or mad. We have all witnessed individuals who go from zero to a hundred quickly, and the default emotion is anger—there is no in-between. We have much more depth than these three emotions.

Many of us lack the language to describe our emotions thoroughly, which can hinder our development and job performance. Developing the ability to connect with our feelings is essential for leadership. It's also vital to examine the guidance the Bible provides about knowledge and wisdom in life. The Holy Spirit is meant to direct us—how can we open ourselves to its influence to comprehend our surroundings?

Imagine if we worked to expand our emotional vocabulary. What would it be like to say we felt "appreciated," "connected," or "respected" when we felt satisfied? Rather than just saying, "I'm mad!" what if we said we felt "annoyed," "displeased," "irritated," or "impatient"? If we're afraid, why not say we feel "panicked," "terrified," or "worried"? These words convey distinct emotions. As leaders, broadening our emotional vocabulary is crucial, especially since we all interpret things differently.[3]

We have all seen people on television do something that's "out of character" for that role. The person usually goes straight to action without taking time to truly analyze why they felt the way they did.

When you are experiencing discomfort, this is not the time for resolution. It's the time to unpack your feelings—where do you feel the discomfort in your body? What emotions are you experiencing? What do you need? It's the time to sit still with your feelings. How would our world look if more people regulated and managed their emotions instead of feeling the need to manage and regulate others?

One of my dear friends was incarcerated for five years. We sometimes talked about the people who were in prison with him. He shared about their poor decisions and lack of understanding of the consequences to their actions. I told him I bet many incarcerated people had an issue with impulse control—a challenge resisting the urge to act on a desire to harm oneself or others. We all know leaders in the workplace who do not manage their emotions or impulses well. Many have caused significant harm.

Emotional intelligence in the workplace not only helps us influence our teams for the better; it also helps improve our chances for promotion. Other positive outcomes linked to higher emotional intelligence include enhanced leadership performance, improved job performance, and greater career success within an organization.[4]

Our emotions play an important role in connecting us to other people. Recognizing our own and others' emotions is a fundamental way we affirm each other. It lays the groundwork for our self-image and how we relate to others.[5]

MAKING MEANING AND PSYCHOLOGICAL CAPITAL

An author I admire, Robert Kegan, asserts that meaning is the primary human emotion.[6] He explains that our brains are designed to find patterns and create meaning from the information we take in through our senses.[7] But we all make meaning differently. Without a shared language, we can easily misconstrue others' intentions. Hochschild notes that each culture has its own emotional dictionary.[8] I recall during a visit to India seeing people nod their heads as if excitedly agreeing.

However, a friend pulled me aside and clarified this meant acknowledgment rather than agreement. Without that knowledge, I could have interpreted this incorrectly.

Like social capital, psychological capital is a resource we can acquire. Psychological capital refers to (1) having the confidence to take on challenging tasks and putting in the effort needed to succeed, (2) maintaining a positive mindset (optimism) about accomplishing goals both now and in the future, (3) persisting toward objectives and, if necessary, changing approaches to achieve them (hope), and (4) when faced with problems and setbacks, overcoming and bouncing back or even beyond to ultimately succeed (resilience).[9]

Emotional intelligence and psychological capital are similar but not the same. Emotional intelligence involves managing and understanding your emotions and those of others, while psychological capital is the application of emotional intelligence. With psychological capital, your worldview and perception of others are positive due to your ability to manage your emotions.

SELF-REFLECTION IN EMOTIONAL INTELLIGENCE

Self-reflection is a key component of emotional intelligence. Here are a few types of self-reflection to consider:[10]

- Narrative critical self-reflection involves reflecting on our own personal journey and beliefs about a situation. It's paying attention to the story we tell ourselves and our assumptions.
- Systemic critical self-reflection goes beyond examining our own assumptions to considering the broader cultural and organizational influences that shape our perspectives in the workplace. It's reflecting on how the culture and systems around us affect the way we and others see things.
- Therapeutic critical self-reflection means taking time to understand our emotional reactions and their impacts, rather than just

reacting. It involves asking ourselves "so what?" questions to get to the root of our feelings, such as anger, betrayal, or sadness.

As leaders, we can make space for self-reflection and create feedback loops to enable course correction. For example, we can use team meetings for growth and development rather than just status updates. With my virtual team, we read and discussed a chapter each week from a relevant book to facilitate bonding and mutual understanding, since we rarely met face-to-face. Practicing self-reflection and providing space for our teams to do so can strengthen emotional intelligence. This is not just something that happens during evaluations and through surveys. It has to be a part of a leader's personal practice.

God provides guidance on managing emotions and relationships through Scripture. Here are some verses that can assist us in strengthening our ability to handle emotions wisely.

Emotionally intelligent leaders read the room before responding. According to Romans 12:17-21, if someone has wronged us, we don't seek revenge. Matthew 18:15-17 advises that if a fellow believer causes harm, we should approach them directly to discuss and resolve the issue. They may listen and make amends, and we can reconcile. However, if they refuse to listen, we should bring one or two unbiased people to mediate so there are witnesses and accountability, and we can try for resolution again.

Likewise, in the workplace, if someone offends you, go to them directly using "I feel" statements to share your perspective and allowing them to respond. If that fails, involve a trusted coworker or HR to help address the situation. But it's crucial to try resolving it yourself with the individual first.

Emotionally intelligent leaders understand that they cannot change people. As leaders, our role is not to change our team members. Rather, we help guide each individual to become the person God intended them to be. This requires that we understand our staff on a personal level. While they may hold worldviews that differ from ours, our aim is to love and exemplify behavior that reflects our Christian faith. As Romans 15:7 says, "Accept one another, even as Christ also accepted you, to the glory of God."

Emotionally intelligent leaders listen to those with wisdom. We can build emotional intelligence by learning from people who demonstrate emotional regulation. The goal is not to seek those who suppress their emotions, masking their pain in silence. Rather, we want to find individuals who deal with their emotions in a healthy, positive way. Ask others how they have developed self-awareness and empathy for others. We should never be too proud to request guidance and help (see Proverbs 13:10). Many of us have heard the saying that we have two ears and one mouth because we should listen more than we speak. Emotionally intelligent leaders ask clarifying questions. "Let every man be swift to hear, slow to speak, and slow to anger; for the anger of man doesn't produce the righteousness of God" (James 1:19-20).

Emotionally intelligent people observe people. When I was in a previous job, my team completed an evaluation to determine our behavior during times of success versus times of stress. It proved incredibly beneficial because it helped me better understand how to support my team members. One employee exhibited identical responses whether she was at ease or under duress. Her consistency was perplexing at first since I couldn't tell when she felt overburdened. But I learned that there was a distinctive look in her eyes signaling the shift between the two states. Without closely observing her amid the hustle and bustle of our work, I risked losing her. I needed to recognize this to ensure her success. As leaders it is important to study our team members. We are stewarding them to walk into their God-given destiny, and without an understanding of who they are, it's difficult to make progress toward that goal.

Emotionally intelligent people understand their emotions, especially their triggers. In one of my favorite books, *Leadership for the Disillusioned,* author Amanda Sinclair examines the leaders of Enron and WorldCom, two major corporations that collapsed due to unprincipled and power-hungry leadership. Sinclair documents the difficult upbringings of these leaders and shows that because they did not address the wounds of their pasts, they recreated a narrative that wrecked the lives of thousands.[11] They were unaware of what triggered them, which is common among leaders who lack self-awareness. Ecclesiastes 7:9 states, "Don't be hasty in your spirit to be angry, for anger rests in the bosom of fools." Anger has damaged many leaders because they did not take time to think, pray, and respond.

Emotionally intelligent leaders embrace humility. Leaders must be open to criticism. Many are arrogant, and they surround themselves with people who inflate their egos. This is perilous. We require individuals in our circle who don't just applaud us but who provide constructive feedback. It's vital that we resist taking offense, listen attentively, and make amendments.

> Pride goes before destruction,
> and an arrogant spirit before a fall.
> It is better to be of a lowly spirit with the poor,
> than to divide the plunder with the proud. (Proverbs 16:18-19)

Leadership requires humility. This doesn't mean we don't have expectations of others or that we don't hold them accountable, but it does mean we recognize the gifts and value of those we work with. We are partners not superiors. When we invest in our teams, establishing a vision with clear, measurable goals and open communication, our potential for success is limitless. As Jesus said, "If I then, the Lord and the Teacher, have washed your feet, you also ought to wash one another's feet. For I have given you an example, that you should also do as I have done to you. Most certainly I tell you, a servant is not greater than his lord, neither is one who is sent greater than he who sent him. If you know these things, blessed are you if you do them" (John 13:14-17). Jesus, the ultimate leader, is the model of humility and service.

Jesus knew he had power and authority as a leader. But he did not abuse this power. Instead he used his influence to encourage others and inspire them to use their God-given gifts and talents. I think some leaders have trouble supporting the success of others because their own unhealed wounds and insecurities make it difficult for them to see the potential in others. Strong team members will not flourish under weak leadership. If your team is having problems, you may need to reflect on your leadership approach, how you see your team, and your understanding of power.

TAPPING INTO SPIRITUAL CAPITAL

Spiritual capital is also a vital element for our success as leaders. Spiritual capital refers to the inner wealth we gain by connecting with our deepest values, purposes, and motivations and integrating these into our lives and work. There are several components of spiritual capital:[12]

- Spiritual sensitivity involves being aware of and attentive to spiritual matters.
- Spiritual leadership means adopting values, attitudes, and behaviors that intrinsically motivate oneself and others to experience meaning, purpose, understanding, and appreciation in their lives.
- Spiritual survival refers to maintaining a sense of purpose and calling, along with the need for social belonging and connection.
- Spiritual outreach means developing and using abilities to positively influence the spiritual condition of others, such as through spiritual gifts.
- Spiritual motivation involves feeling divinely inspired to fulfill one's purpose or work.

Spiritual capital is not just available to individuals; organizations can also possess many of these qualities, especially those of us working in service-related fields like nonprofit management or ministry. As leaders we can exemplify these traits even within companies that are not faith-based. Organizations with high spiritual capital nurture their teams and are attentive to their emotional needs. They prioritize supporting employees, fostering relationships, and providing safe environments for their staff. These organizations also emphasize intellectual growth for their teams, encouraging professional development opportunities. Furthermore, they cultivate inspirational settings where employees feel hopeful that their work has meaning and purpose. How are you growing these elements of spiritual capital in your life and work?

EMOTIONAL LABOR IN THE WORKPLACE

As women of color, we must be mindful not to suppress our own emotions while taking on the burdens and emotional work of others. A study by Catalyst, a nonprofit focused on building inclusive work environments for women, analyzes this issue using the term "emotional tax."[13] This refers to an amplified feeling of being unlike your coworkers due to your gender, race, or ethnicity. It also refers to the negative impacts this can have on health, wellness, and the capacity to prosper at work.

Theresa Suico authored an insightful article called "Emotional Labor and Women of Color in the Workplace: A Reality Check," in which she explains how women of color feel pressure to regulate their emotional expressions when interacting with others at work.[14] Women of color already deal with many challenges, including racism, sexism, classism, and the constant struggle to be valued for their contributions. Having to additionally manage others' feelings about them compounds existing struggles. Suico portrays the burden women of color confront:

> I interact with customers and colleagues alike in a premeditated regimen of behavior, designed over the years to elicit a maximally favorable response from those I interact with. If this approach seems a tad too cautious or calculated, trust me—I really would have preferred to walk in the world differently.[15]

Carolyn West links Black women's experiences with emotional labor to the "Mammy" stereotype deeply embedded in American culture. Mammy was a character in *Gone with the Wind* who catered to the White family's needs. West explains that the expectation for Black women to constantly provide service with a smile persists today. Indeed, Black women across all professions, from corporate employees to service workers, lament that colleagues and managers expect them to take on caretaker roles like counselors, nannies, and therapists.[16]

Many women of color experience internal turmoil when parts of their cultural identity are invalidated.[17] Feeling disconnected in this way erodes self-esteem. "Emotional dissonance clearly indicates emotional labor because of the huge effort and restraint required to show an emotional facade that conflicts with real feelings."[18]

So how do you handle a workplace that is devoid of resources to support who you are? You'll need to employ your emotional and spiritual resilience by leaning into your relationship with God. Develop a spiritual practice of prayer, fellowship with other believers, and Bible study. In my own prayer life, I'm trying not to just tell God what I want and need but to create space to hear from God. It's also important to get support from others—tell people what you need. Too many of us walk around telling people we are fine when we are not fine. Find meaning outside of work. Your identity cannot be tied to what you do. If necessary, find an executive coach or a therapist to help. I have met too many leaders who have allowed the pain of work to suppress their voice and creativity. Your peace is important and feeds your power. Suffering in silence cannot become a new normal.

SCRIPTURES TO CONSIDER

> But the fruit of the Spirit is love, joy, peace, patience, kindness, goodness, faith, gentleness, and self-control. Against such things there is no law. (Galatians 5:22-23)

> Better a patient person than a warrior,
>   one with self-control than one who takes a city.
>   (Proverbs 16:32 NIV)

In nothing be anxious, but in everything, by prayer and petition with thanksgiving, let your requests be made known to God. And the peace of God, which surpasses all understanding, will guard your hearts and your thoughts in Christ Jesus. (Philippians 4:6-7)

QUESTIONS FOR REFLECTION

1. In what ways do you make time for self-reflection and processing your thoughts and feelings on a regular basis?
2. Are there instances in your work where you feel obligated to regulate your emotions for the benefit of others? How might you establish healthy boundaries around emotional labor for the sake of your own well-being?
3. What methods can you utilize to increase your emotional intelligence, psychological capital, and spiritual capital? In what ways would cultivating these characteristics affect your ability to lead effectively?

PRAYER

God, my feelings play a big role in how I behave. I pray today that you will help me manage my emotions as they come up. Instead of responding with anger, hatred, jealousy, spite, and arrogance, fill me with your comforting love, tranquility, serenity, and empathy. With these virtues guiding me, I will go out today and do kind deeds for others. In Jesus' name, amen.

PROFILES IN LEADERSHIP

The Triumph of Tina: Tina's Story

Tina is in her late twenties. A Latina, she became involved in the community quickly after college. She worked at a major organization and quickly moved up the ladder. Things changed after the pandemic and her role in the organization changed. "In late 2020, once everyone had gotten their routine down, there was a lot of harm being done in the sense that organizations weren't fully being transparent with their employees," she says. "They were causing harm and there was a lot of internal ego."

As funding dropped, she saw "mostly women, women of color, and young Black and Brown people let go. That made me realize we can be talking the talk, but we're definitely not walking the walk." Tina became disheartened.

"My mental health became so debilitating that my doctor asked me to take days off work because my entire face had broken out in a rash," Tina says. "My health was declining. My mental health was declining. My doctor told me I couldn't live alone anymore. I needed to go home because I needed to be cared for."

Tina did not receive support from the organization. She was told she couldn't take days off because she didn't have multiple doctors' notes explaining why. "Never had I been told I needed a doctor's note to take a day off," she says. "It started to feel like they were trying to get me out of the organization."

Tina had a great relationship with her CEO, but she experienced intimidation from other male leaders. "I had to leave the organization because it had become toxic and detrimental to my health," she says. She later found out that leaving was the straw that broke the camel's back. Things finally changed because the group feared losing other great leaders. This was a wonderful outcome, but she wondered why people had to be harmed in the process of the organization learning to value its leaders.

Race and gender have played a role in Tina's journey. "I think race has always been on the forefront of my mind," she says. "When you have a darker complexion, you're racialized. I went to high school in a predominantly White setting, so I felt it constantly. When I got to college, I was around a lot of White folks there too. And then I found my crowd once I started taking courses on race. I was able to make friends in those classes. That transformed my understanding of race and finally gave me vocabulary for what I had been experiencing."

Current events also defined the role of race in Tina's life. "I graduated in 2012 from high school," she says. "That's when Trayvon Martin was murdered. I was absolutely radicalized at that time because I was seeing someone who was my age."

Tina believes in intentionally naming the harm being done by different communities: anti-Blackness, misogyny, patriarchy, white supremacy. "Those things are very uncomfortable for people, which is probably also why people are a little bit afraid of me," she says. "So I tend to be silly and have fun. But I do like to be a truth-teller. I pride myself on that."

Being a Latina leader is difficult in ways Tina had not imagined it would be. "I've gotten more support from Black women than my own community," she says. "I think that probably has everything to do with the fact that I'm naming anti-Blackness and white supremacy and these uncomfortable things. . . . It is vital that people confront their ego and their beliefs and hope for a better society outside of themselves."

Tina's background is rooted in the Catholic church but she is not a practicing Catholic. "Honestly, I was turned off by a lot of what I experienced in the Catholic church," she says. "Disconnecting from the church allowed my spirituality to grow in new ways. I found a better path by becoming an all-encompassing spiritual person who is rooted in my ancestors and my belief in people and love."

She experienced hurt in church, as many of us have. "I've had to unpack a lot of that," Tina says. "I practice healing work and intentional care work. . . . Experiencing a boxed-in version of religion at a young age helped me open my mind and connect with people on a path that's a lot bigger than the one-faith path created for me."

Lessons for Younger Women

- "Listen to your gut and do not settle. Know how powerful you are, know how capable you are, know how worthy you are, because we do not have to accept harm as a norm. We are allowed to

- speak up for ourselves, even in these institutions that are our full-time employers."
- "We spend so much time as workers that we have to demand more. We're allowed to demand more. We're allowed to demand a better work environment. We're allowed to ask for a raise. We're allowed to fight for what we believe in because the majority of our time is spent at work. . . . I encourage everyone to keep demanding more and keep going to where we find a place that feels better for us."
- "I would love to see a huge shift in American capitalism that lets people enjoy their lives more, rest more, heal more, and transform more. How as a society do we go from focusing on work to focusing on ourselves, our families, our passions, our trips, our dreams, our hopes? I want us to lean into what that might look like, because we're on this earth for more than just work."

Dealing with Racism, Sexism, and Other "Isms"

- "Stay rooted in the people, stay rooted in the truth and love and care. We often get excited about dealing with trauma through accolades. It's great to be in a newspaper or on TV. But none of that has healed my wounds. None of that has paid my bills."
- "We have to stay grounded in the movement for people and for liberation. Encompassing that with radical care, love, and truth allows us to stay rooted in the work of the people."
- "Healing connection is the most powerful thing that can happen between people, whether it's through communication or art or writing. Staying committed to creating art and work for all of us and not just myself has allowed me to keep growing and to stay rooted in what I hope will be a long, revolutionary life."

9

Discrimination in the Workplace

When I was in my late twenties, I got the opportunity to teach full time at Jarvis Christian College in East Texas. It was my lifelong dream to build a career as a college professor, and this was my chance. At the time I was living in Irving, Texas, near Dallas, with my then-husband, and we agreed this was an opportunity I simply could not turn down, despite the distance. So I began commuting over a hundred miles to teach in Hawkins and Tyler. I stayed in an apartment in Tyler during the week, and on weekends I went back home to Irving to be with my husband. Some weekends I would also travel to Louisiana to visit my parents, since Tyler was halfway between Dallas and northern Louisiana. Though it required a lot of commuting, I was thrilled to finally be teaching full time in my field after having had only part-time teaching jobs before.

I became pregnant with our daughter soon after. I worried at first about how having a child would affect my career goals, but three months into the pregnancy, my health suffered and we feared losing the baby. My doctor advised me to stop traveling so much and take time off to rest. I had envisioned having a midwife and water birth, but my gynecologist referred me to a high-risk pregnancy doctor instead. Despite these challenges, I managed to finish the school year. I was thrilled to be voted outstanding new professor, outstanding college professor, and receive another student award in the midst of such difficulty. I was doing what I loved and sharing it with others. As soon as the school year ended, I moved back home. I realized my dreams would still come true, just in a different way than I had imagined.

I applied for a dean position at a local community college, wearing an oversized dress to conceal my pregnancy. During the final round of interviews, the panel's enthusiasm came to an abrupt end when I disclosed that I would be having a baby in a few months. As you can imagine, I was not offered the job. After that experience, I worried that motherhood would be seen as an impediment to excelling at both work and home.

My dear friend Comfort Brown allowed me to work with her at a summer camp and told me about an open position as a director at St. Philip's School and Community Center. Because of my previous experience, I wore an even larger dress to hide my pregnancy, hoping I could get past the first interview. If I impressed the hiring manager with my experience and intellect, maybe my pregnancy would not be considered an obstacle. Dr. Terry Flowers offered me the job and let me know he was aware I was pregnant and that he was the father of three daughters himself. I was relieved.

Though I had planned to begin my new position right away, I was ordered to go on bed rest due to complications with my pregnancy. These complications led to an even more troublesome delivery. I was diagnosed with toxemia, and I pleaded with my doctor not to hospitalize me. I had to inform Dr. Flowers about this situation, and I was sure I would lose the job. But Dr. Flowers waited for me patiently from June to October, when I could finally start work. This is highly unusual in the professional world, and to this day, I have tremendous respect and affection for this Dallas icon who provided me an opportunity when so many doors had closed. While I cannot claim I was a victim of pregnancy discrimination, I recognize that for many, this part of our life experience can be weaponized against us.

WOMEN AND PREGNANCY DISCRIMINATION

Despite the Pregnancy Discrimination Act of 1978, which amended the Civil Rights Act to prohibit discrimination based on pregnancy, childbirth, or related conditions, pregnancy discrimination still exists. This is true even in "at-will" employment states like Texas, where employers can fire employees for any reason or no reason at all, as long as it's not illegal.[1] But it's challenging for individuals to prove they were fired because of illegal, discriminatory reasons, and the process can take a long time. So pregnancy discrimination persists, even with legal protections in place.

According to research from the National Partnership for Women and Families, close to 31,000 pregnancy discrimination complaints were filed with the Equal Employment Opportunity Commission and similar state agencies from 2010 to 2015.[2] The data shows that while White women accounted for 46% of the complaints, African American women were disproportionately impacted, filing 29% of complaints while only making up 14% of the female workforce. As I experienced in my own pregnancy, it is common for Black women to face complications like preterm delivery, preeclampsia, and high blood pressure disorders at higher rates than other groups.[3] These health concerns can negatively affect Black women's ability to remain employed and insured during pregnancy. In summary, while pregnancy discrimination affects women broadly, women of color bear an unequal burden, facing both higher rates of workplace discrimination and pregnancy-related health complications.

Let me provide some more detail about what these complications looked like in my own life. In addition to developing toxemia and cholestasis, a liver dysfunction, during pregnancy, my delivery was also difficult. I labored from Tuesday evening until Thursday evening then finally underwent a cesarean section because I was unable to dilate fully. At last our daughter Kazai Kiara was born.

I was happy to have the support of my mother and the nurses during the first three days of my daughter's life. But when I was discharged from the hospital, my mother left for Louisiana to help my father, and my husband only had a week off to assist me. Despite my doula's attempts to help me breastfeed, Kazai was not latching and I was not producing milk. My six-week maternity leave became eight weeks. I was finally cleared by my doctor to return to work, still healing and trying to find reliable childcare. Kazai had reflux, and dealing with a sick baby while starting a new job was nerve racking. I was exhausted because she was not sleeping through the night. I did not have the option to stay home because we had already used up savings and a 401(k).

Once in my new director role, I found that most of my team members were older than my parents. It was challenging to learn the work, get to know my team, and stay on top of everything with a new baby. On top of that, there was drama with my child's daycare and I had to start interviewing new providers. Childcare consumed a large part of our income.

Balancing the demands of work, motherhood, marriage, and personal time was not easy, and many women encounter similar challenges. We juggle numerous responsibilities, attempting to keep all the balls in motion. Frankly, we work multiple shifts: the typical nine-to-five job, plus extra work duties, home and parenting tasks, a beauty regimen, and, for women of color, racism and discrimination issues. This balancing act is a common struggle for women as we strive to manage career, family, self-care, and societal pressures.

WORK, HOME, AND MOTHERHOOD

According to the World Economic Forum, women work almost one hour longer per day than men when paid and unpaid work are considered.[4] Plus, many women have two jobs. Data from the Bureau of Labor Statistics shows that in 2019, 8.1 million US workers held more than one job, and over half of these were women. The percentage of women holding multiple jobs, at 5.6%, was higher than that of men, at 4.7%.

These extra work hours become an even more significant factor in women's lives when you consider the challenges they face in the workplace, such as sexual harassment, pay inequity, and lack of advancement opportunities. A 2021 study found that despite having the talent, ambition, confidence, and determination to succeed, women of color receive insufficient support from leaders who could help them advance.[5] The "glass ceiling" is a misnomer for women of color—"concrete ceiling" better describes the barriers they confront.

McKinsey & Company and LeanIn.org's seventh annual Women in the Workplace report shows that the pandemic exacerbated women's workplace challenges. When compared with men, women leaders are 63% more likely to provide emotional support, 31% more likely to address burnout, 21% more likely to help with work-life issues, and 17% more likely to ensure manageable workloads.[6] These additional responsibilities are unpaid and unacknowledged atop an already heavy workload. When I left my job at St. Philip's after five years, my role had to be split among more than five people!

I must admit, it was tough balancing my home and work life. As much as I wanted a spotless home, there were times I had to accept that the dishes would stay in the sink until the next day. The women who came before me in my family also balanced motherhood and work. Both my grandmothers worked as maids for White families during a time of limited options. When I was a little girl, my mother worked at Western Electric (now AT&T) and had to be at work by 6 a.m. My aunts, cousins, and friends' mothers did the same. The ability to stay home was a luxury none of us could afford.

Still, I felt inadequate for a long time because my home did not look like a Martha Stewart magazine layout. I did not understand how my mother could work, come home to cook and clean, and then get us ready for bed. But then my mother said something profound that changed my outlook forever. She said her job in the seventies and eighties did not require the brain capacity I had to use. I was not just physically tired. By the time the day was over, I was mentally drained as well, only to wake up and repeat the routine.

When my daughter was born in 2000, childcare cost almost $800 per week, which was prohibitively expensive for the time. More recently, a friend had to withdraw her kids from daycare because it cost over $2,000 monthly for two children. When my child was three, I was fortunate to work at a school that allowed me to have her with me until age eight, when I left the role. Still, managing afterschool care along with staff, volunteers, and budgets was demanding. I remember working late one day when my then four-year-old daughter slapped her hand on my desk and said "Momma, it's time to go home." From then on I had to carefully schedule my time to balance work and getting her home for dinner, reading, and bedtime while maintaining our household.

Because let's face it: women take on a "second shift" at home. Women who work full time, have a partner, and have children say they spend a total of 71 hours per week taking care of children, caring for elderly relatives, and doing household chores. In comparison, men report spending 51 hours per week on these tasks. Three-quarters of Black and Latina women spend more than 21 hours per week on housework, while just over half of White women spend this much time on household chores. Black and Latina women also tend to spend more time than White women on caring for children and elderly family members.[7]

During the pandemic, the lines between work life and home life became unclear for many women. With remote work and schooling, women often did not have a chance to stop working and be free from their responsibilities. The usual separation between professional work and domestic duties was lost when everything blended together at home. Many women no longer had the opportunity to clock out from their job or take a break from household and childcare tasks. The pandemic eliminated the transition time women used to have between their workday and personal life, and many of these tensions continue in the present day.

THE BEAUTY SHIFT

Social media places immense pressure on women to achieve an unattainable standard of beauty. When I was pregnant with my daughter Kazai, I gained over fifty pounds. Although I lost some of the weight afterward, I regained a portion of it due to the stresses of work and life. I was unable to exercise right after giving birth because of my C-section, which was frustrating. I also struggled to manage high blood pressure resulting from the pregnancy. Women are frequently judged on their looks, impacting intimate relationships and work. One study found that physically attractive people earn higher incomes than average.[8]

Jennifer Haskin notes that for women with children, there is an additional "beauty shift" on top of their work and home responsibilities. Drawing on Naomi Wolf's *The Beauty Myth*, Haskin makes the following points: (1) Most women feel compelled to meet cultural standards of beauty and femininity. (2) Achieving the "right" appearance takes time, money, and emotional investment. (3) The work involved in meeting beauty norms includes not just visible grooming habits but also unseen thought processes, choices, and behaviors. (4) While some beauty routines may be compartmentalized, much of this labor overlaps with women's other responsibilities throughout the day.[9] In summary, women's social opportunities can depend heavily on conforming to expected beauty ideals.

Societal beauty standards tend to place higher regard on Whiteness. Generations of women of color have altered their appearance through products and clothing, hoping it would result in opportunities in the workplace. They may straighten their hair, use bleaching products to lighten their skin, or minimize the appearance of large hips.

White normativity and standards of beauty affect all women of color, especially in who "looks like a leader" and gets favored or promoted. Black women especially face beauty-standards discrimination when it comes to our hair. Dove's CROWN Research Study found that Black women are 1.5 times more likely than others to be sent home from work over their hair.[10] The study also showed that Black women's hairstyles are more heavily policed in the workplace and are often viewed as less professional. In 2019, Dove and the CROWN Coalition partnered with California State Senator Holly J. Mitchell to create the CROWN Act, which aims to protect against discrimination based on race-based hairstyles. The act extends legal protection to hair textures and styles like braids, locs, twists, and knots in workplaces and public schools.

But for many years, Black women straightened their hair to conform to societal beauty standards. I was no exception, using harsh chemical relaxers that caused severe damage and hair loss. This forced me to cut my hair very short, and ultimately I transitioned to my natural texture. The chemicals used in relaxers and other hair products aimed at Black women—substances like cyclosiloxanes, nonylphenols, and phthalates—are extremely toxic. Research links these chemicals to hormone disruption, infertility, asthma, fibroids, and cancer risk. The health and environmental impacts are too high, so we must find safer, more inclusive beauty practices.[11] Attempting to conform can have consequences beyond limiting job opportunities; it can also have a negative impact on our health.

THE SHIFT OF RACISM AND DISCRIMINATION

The racism and discrimination endured by women of color often exacerbate the many challenges they already face. Chronic stress from lifelong discrimination takes a toll on health. Studies by Harvard's School of Public Health reveal that Black women suffer health risks from both biased health care providers who dismiss their concerns and from the biological effects of unrelenting stress.[12] This stress, called "weathering," contributes significantly to hypertension and diabetes in African Americans, Native Hawaiians, Latin Americans, and other marginalized groups, according to research by Dr. Arline Geronimus.[13] She explains that people of color endure repeated stressors across their lifespans, often peaking in early to middle adulthood, which increases their vulnerability to health issues overall.

While the stresses of racial and gender discrimination can take a heavy toll and leave us feeling overwhelmed, there are ways to cope and find support:

1. ***Do not suffer alone.*** Build a community that affirms who you are. Friends and family who understand your challenges can provide critical support. I could not survive without my loved ones lifting me up.
2. ***Seek health care providers with experience serving diverse communities.*** While shared identity is not essential, your doctor must grasp the unique needs of people of color. Dr. Jill Waggoner saved my health by recognizing I required care beyond the typical approach. Thanks to her expertise and commitment, she caught a thyroid issue multiple doctors had overlooked. With a provider who sees and understands you, potentially dire health consequences can be averted.
3. ***Find a therapist.*** A therapist can provide valuable insight and support. We all carry trauma from experiences in our workplaces and families. By addressing past hurts and formative influences with a skilled therapist's guidance, we can gain new understanding that was previously obscured. This process of healing often involves unlearning ingrained patterns.
4. ***Ask for help.*** In the beginning, I strived to do it all, believing that needing help made me less of a woman. But trying to be "Superwoman" was not only overwhelming, it took a serious toll on my mental and physical health. Though I could not afford a weekly housekeeper early in my career, monthly help still provided relief. If you need assistance with household tasks, do not hesitate to ask family, friends, or social services for support. You don't have to do everything alone.

5. *Relish your beauty.* You have inner and outer beauty. Altering your appearance with harsh chemicals or extreme measures can have lasting consequences. Consider connecting with natural hair groups like Nappturality that offer organic products and support for embracing your natural beauty.

God wants us to know our value as women, as mothers, as workers.

SCRIPTURES TO CONSIDER

There is neither Jew nor Greek, there is neither slave nor free man, there is neither male nor female; for you are all one in Christ Jesus. (Galatians 3:28)

But Yahweh said to Samuel, "Don't look on his face, or on the height of his stature, because I have rejected him; for I don't see as man sees. For man looks at the outward appearance, but Yahweh looks at the heart." (1 Samuel 16:7)

God created man in his own image. In God's image he created him; male and female he created them. (Genesis 1:27)

QUESTIONS FOR REFLECTION

1. Describe your typical work schedule. What are your "shifts"?
2. How do you practice self-care in your daily life? Are there any new healthy habits you'd like to try adopting? What might those look like for you?
3. In a society that often pressures people to conform, what are some ways you express your individuality and stay true to yourself?

PRAYER

Dear God, you created me in your image as an original and unique individual. My value comes from you, as you formed me with care and purpose, making no mistakes. My inner and outer beauty will never fade, and like the Virtuous Woman, I have much to contribute beyond mere appearance. May your radiance shine through me. In Jesus' name, amen.

PROFILES IN LEADERSHIP

Knowing Your Superpowers: Janie's Story

Janie is an Asian woman in her early forties who is an entrepreneur. She grew up with a supportive family and a mom who was influential in molding her leadership style. Janie's journey is one to celebrate, yet she feels tokenized. One of the most challenging experiences she's had in the workplace was dealing with an Asian male who had a similar background. Initially, he was supportive and then things changed. He became threatened by her leadership. This experience prompted her to start her own company.

The challenges Janie faced have been mostly at the hands of men. Her journey has taught her that "men of color still have more privileges." Faith has been central to her journey, and Janie states that it has made her more resilient in the face of opposition and rejection: "Success grounds my level of humility and degree of deep gratitude even more. I'm radically genuine and truthfully authentic, and that throws people for a loop sometimes."

Lessons for Younger Women

- "Be aware of your surroundings. If people show you their true colors, believe them."
- "I refuse to let my vulnerable compassionate leadership be viewed as a weakness in business."

Dealing with Racism, Sexism, and other "Isms"

- "Know your superpower."
- "Kill them with kindness—it's my superpower."

10

The Postracial Society Is an Ideal

I NEVER THOUGHT I WOULD WITNESS a year like 2008 in my lifetime. I knew a Black person becoming president was a possibility; I just never thought I would see it happen. I think of my grandparents, who did not live to witness President Obama or Vice President Kamala Harris achieve office, dying with the belief that no one of color could ever be in the Oval Office.

Once Obama was elected, a belief floated through civil discourse around the idea of a postracial society. The view was that America no longer had racism. The election of a Black man as president demonstrated that the country had grown beyond the cancer that once dominated so many areas of life. We were finally accomplishing Dr. King's dream of a society where Black and White children held hands and were treated equally.

In theory, this is an aspiration. In reality, America continues to deal with the issue of race that has permeated this country since its founding. The outcry against Nikole Hannah Jones's 1619 Project, a major *New York Times* feature about the history of US enslavement,[1] illustrates the difficulty American society has regarding its founding and the place of race in this country's history.

Despite the many advances for people of color in America, there is still much work to be done if we are to achieve true equity and equality.

Police shootings of Black people are much higher than for any other group, with 6.2 fatalities per million annually between 2015 and 2024.[2] People of color have been targeted in education and in the workplace. During the pandemic, a third of Asian Americans feared they would be harmed.[3] Challenges exist in health care, housing, and other social determinants of health. Consider the following data points:[4]

- In 2022, nonelderly American Indian and Alaska Native (AIAN) and Latino individuals were more than twice as likely to be uninsured compared to their White counterparts.
- Among adults with mental health conditions, a lower percentage of Latino, Black, and Asian adults accessed mental health services compared to White adults in the same year.
- As of 2022, life expectancy was shorter for AIAN individuals (67.9 years) and Black individuals (72.8 years) compared to White individuals (77.5 years).
- Additionally, AIAN, Latino, and Black populations experienced more significant declines in life expectancy from 2019 to 2022 than White individuals.

In terms of housing discrimination, a local Black developer remarked to me that the lack of diverse appraisers in the housing industry has a direct impact on property values. Properties located in predominantly Black neighborhoods are undervalued by an average of $48,000 each, resulting in a total loss of approximately $156 billion for those owners. Black, Native American, and Latino households often consist of low-income renters with incomes at or below the poverty line, or 30% of the median income for their area as compared to Whites.[5] Many of these issues correlate directly with systemic racism. Racism is embedded in policies, structures, and laws. In our willingness as a society to move beyond the past to a postracial society, we would be irresponsible not to recognize the role of the past on the present.

As we have already discussed, racism is also rampant in the workplace. In 2023, the number of discrimination cases reported to the Equal Employment Opportunity Commission grew by 10.3% over the prior year, and the agency investigated more than 80,000 claims.[6] Sixty percent of women indicate they have experienced discrimination based on gender, while 33% report facing discrimination due to race.[7] Racism shows up in the workplace both overtly and subtly. Hiring and promotion bias is one example, with Black women receiving promotions at a much lower rate than White women.[8] Asian women are often mistaken for each other in their workplaces and, as a result, their contributions are overlooked. They too have a difficult time being promoted despite receiving positive reviews.[9]

Compensation disparities are common. Latinas are paid approximately 46 percent less than White men and 26 percent less than White women.[10] Black women make 67 cents for each dollar earned by a White male. Over the course of a lifetime, this means Black women are losing out on a million dollars or more.[11] There is a considerable wage disparity in the workforce for Indigenous women as well, with Native women earning 55 cents for every dollar White men make.[12]

Women of color experience microaggressions and overt discrimination in the workplace as well. Microaggressions are subtle, often unconsciously biased comments that diminish people from marginalized groups. For example, complimenting a woman of color for being "articulate" presupposes that her racial group is not typically well-spoken. This happened to me during my college years when a customer at my parents' restaurant was surprised by the way I spoke and assumed I was a teacher. More than 75% of people of color have dealt with microaggressions in the workplace.[13] More overt discrimination involves racial slurs, harassment, and exclusionary practices. Both microaggressions and overt discrimination contribute to hostile work environments for women of color.

One way discrimination shows up is in unfair performance evaluations that have detrimental impacts on employees. These biases lead to unreasonably low ratings, limited promotion opportunities, and a toxic work culture for marginalized groups. I experienced this firsthand when my schedule was scrutinized in reviews while similar flexibility was permitted for White colleagues, despite our identical job duties requiring community engagement. Tokenism is another form of bias; it occurs when organizations hire or promote people of color to create the appearance of inclusion without providing equal opportunities or meaningful participation. This perpetuates stereotypes and undermines real achievements. It creates a narrative that women of color are hired because of programs like affirmative action instead of their qualifications.

In workplaces that lack diversity altogether, organizations often cite a lack of qualified people of color to hire. This problematic claim overlooks the need for inclusive talent development. Establishing apprenticeship, mentoring, and leadership pipeline programs would expand opportunities for leaders of color. As leaders of color ourselves, we must be intentional about fostering the next generation, both informally through mentoring and formally via succession planning. Doing so will build a diverse corps of future leaders.

Organizations frequently overlook how their culture impacts employees, allowing harmful attitudes and behaviors to persist unchecked. These toxic environments alienate people of color, hindering their professional growth. To combat workplace racism, organizations must commit to inclusivity by implementing unbiased hiring and promotions, comprehensive bias training, performance evaluations that encourage teamwork, an inclusive and respectful culture, and amplifying marginalized voices.

AGEISM AND WOMEN OF COLOR IN THE WORKPLACE

We know that gender and racial discrimination are problems in the workplace. If you are also young or old while working, those identities may compound the challenges you experience.

My leadership journey began when I was in my late teens and twenties as a college student at the University of Texas at Arlington. I ran for student leadership roles on campus and found myself as a young Black woman working with adults who had limited experience supporting students of color. One day an admin embarrassed me publicly about the sound of my voice. It was a painful experience—the first of many.

Later, when I was in my twenties, a noted Dallas school board member arrived at an event where I was registering attendees. I was elated to see this woman I knew from the news and looked up to. Unfortunately I mispronounced her name, and instead of seeing my eagerness, she too felt it necessary to publicly embarrass me for my mistake. Some leaders along my career journey were too busy or uninterested in taking time to mentor me, but others saw my potential and took an active role in my life. All these experiences informed the way in which I work. I pride myself on being available to young women because I know how difficult it can be to get a break. As women of color, we have a real opportunity to speak into the lives of young women. We are doing them a disservice when we don't take the time to build our legacy by sharing our lives.

I work with many young women who are in senior leader roles in their thirties, which older women can find threatening. I remind these young women that opportunities were not as readily available to many of us at their age, and I believe we can offer a lot to each other if we remain proximate and create intentional communities of support.

MENSTRUATION AT WORK

A menstrual cycle is a natural part of a woman's life. After I had my daughter, I was told that my cycles would become lighter, which was a lie from the pit of hell. They became unbearable, resulting in severe bleeding that I later discovered was due to fibroids. One day at work I bled through a cloth chair. Not only did I feel bad about ruining the chair, but I messed up my dress. I was blessed to have a male boss who understood and reminded me that he had a wife and three girls. He generously gave me time off to regroup after this experience. But I continued to experience significant pain and blood loss during my cycles. I was anemic at times and fatigued when "Mother Nature" came for a visit. It's hard to focus on your work when you have PMS, cramps, bleeding, and other symptoms. Each woman has a different experience, but we all can agree that it is an experience.

Some companies are experimenting with menstruation leave, but women are often afraid to share their challenges for fear of being seen as less-than, so they suck it up and go to work. The idea of menstruation leave has pros and cons, which scholars Rachel B. Levitt and Jessica L. Barnack-Tavlaris explore. The authors state that until we delve into and eliminate stigmas about gender and menstruation, this kind of leave may have an additional negative impact on women.[14]

LIFE IN THE BODY OF A SEASONED WOMAN OF COLOR

As I've gotten older, I've witnessed the biases women encounter as they age. Although age discrimination laws protect individuals over forty in the workplace, stereotypes too often become a barrier that prevents engaging more seasoned women. I call myself an early fall yard bird instead of a spring chicken. I'm older and I have much to offer, but there is a belief that older populations are not technologically savvy, have health issues, and cost too much. The AARP states, "Two out of three workers between ages 45 and 74 say they have seen or experienced age discrimination at work, and job seekers over age 35 cite it as a top obstacle to getting hired."[15]

For those of us who are aging, our bodies are also going through changes as well. Women typically experience menopause in their midforties through midfifties when they are often in leadership positions at work, which makes it difficult to maintain the role and hide the symptoms they experience. When I was growing up I would hear older women talk about "the change." I never really understood what that meant, and my impression of menopause was negative. It was a sign of getting old, not something to be embraced as a beautiful transition in life. As I've entered this stage, I've seen it as God's way of reminding me that although I cannot birth children, I have the opportunity to birth something different—my destiny.

Menopause is not something that has been discussed until recently in the workplace. The Mayo Clinic conducted a study of over four thousand women to study the impact of menopause symptoms, discovering that these symptoms affected not just workplace productivity but the national economy.[16] As one *Time* magazine writer said, "$26.6 billion is being lost due to productivity declines and health care expenses."[17] The majority of the women in the study were White, but the researchers found that Black women and Latinas experience menopause earlier, have more severe symptoms, and report negative experiences in the workplace as a result of their menopausal symptoms. Symptoms cause disruptions for women both physically and mentally, ranging from mood swings to brain fog, lack of sleep to hot flashes and night sweats. For Black women, stress due to weathering and the impact of structural racism play a role in the severity of menopause symptoms.

Another challenge is lack of treatment for women of color; doctors tend to believe they can tolerate the pain of menopause and may even dismiss them outright.[18] My mother says that as she gets older, she feels increasingly ignored and dismissed by health care providers because of her age. I wish as a society we could see this phase as something special in our lives marked by rituals and ceremonies.

Whether young or old, it's important that women of color recognize the life cycle of our bodies. We must advocate for our bodies and needs and talk about these life changes with each other. I wish I had known what to expect. My experience with menopause is much different from my mother's. She wasn't given the information or tools she needed to navigate it, and I'm learning as I go along. I'm grateful to amazing physicians like Dr. Jessica Shepherd and Dr. Jill Waggoner, who have been phenomenal guides on this journey of discovery. Educate yourself, and when you are not receiving the support you need, don't give up on yourself—keep fighting for the help you need. You deserve it!

STICKING TOGETHER IS A NECESSITY

For a woman of color in the workplace, it can be exhausting to deal with microaggressions, racism, pay disparities, and all the other issues we face. It's important to create safe spaces to refuel and protect yourself when faced with these obstacles. If you are a leader, what can you do to make spaces safe for those under your care?

As women of color, we often focus on racism in the context of dominant culture, but racism exists within communities of color as well. Scholar Eduardo Bonilla-Silva developed the theory of racialized social systems, which examines the hierarchy between ethnic groups. Those higher up receive more opportunities than those who are viewed as less-than. This is compounded by gender and other identities. Various groups can be pitted against one another, which results in more pain than opportunity.[19] How do we make sure as women of color that we are not contributing to the oppression of one another in the workplace? As women of faith, we have a responsibility to remove barriers not just for those like us but for others as well. Our freedom is intertwined—we can all thrive together!

TIPS TO PRESERVE YOUR SANITY IN THE WORKPLACE

Navigating these workplace challenges as a woman of color can feel overwhelming, but there are practical steps you can take to maintain your well-being.

Know the season you are in. Too often, women compare their trajectories to those of others, not being fully aware of the variables involved in a person's journey. We are only aware of what we see. There is a danger in evaluating your life against the perceptions you have of others. I often share with young women that this critical information will save them from the trap of comparison. I can do more in my current season because I am not married, and my child is an adult. Yet, when I was married and with a young child, there were things I didn't have the capacity to accomplish. It had nothing to do with intellect or skill. Some things require time that you may need to allocate to other responsibilities. Your spring season of life will look much different from your winter. Appreciate each because you will miss the beauty in each if you are too busy trying to turn your life into what you see others doing around you.

You need a coach. Consider hiring a professional coach to support your growth and development. A coach provides a safe space for open conversations and accountability, which can be invaluable for reflecting on your current role and planning for future opportunities.

Get a therapist. To promote mental and emotional well-being, consider seeking therapy. We all have past hurts that can resurface when we face difficult work environments. A therapist can help you process old wounds so they don't hinder your health and happiness now and in the days ahead.

Bust a move. Make a commitment to exercise by signing up for classes that engage your body and mind, such as mindfulness, belly dancing, or pickleball. While high intensity interval training (HIIT) is an excellent option, I don't recommend it for beginners. Start slowly when adopting a new exercise regimen.

Make time to exhale. Schedule your vacation well in advance and utilize all of your allotted time off. Don't wait until the last minute—mark it on your calendar now. That's what vacation is for!

Boundaries are your friend. Set clear boundaries with work. Avoid bringing work home if you can. If necessary, designate a specific non-bedroom area for work tasks and set a timer to prevent encroachment on personal life.

Work hard. Play hard. Balance hard work with recreational activities that spark joy, nourish your spirit, and provide respite from job demands. Make time for hobbies and interests outside of work.

Bookend your day with prayer and Bible reading. Incorporate prayer and Bible reading into your daily routine as bookends to the day. Establish a habit of connecting with God both morning and night.

Write in your journal. Set aside time each day for journaling and self-reflection. Just as we build in feedback loops at work, we need them in our personal lives to avoid repeating mistakes. Journaling allows the mind space to ponder, explore, and gain clarity.

As women of color, healing comes from connecting with one another. How can we make time to listen to each other's stories and surround ourselves with people who energize us?

Strive for peace and joy. Our current landscape has so many unknowns. It's so easy to become preoccupied by fear and anxiety about what is to come because of the numerous changes underway in our world. If you spend so much time focusing on what will happen or what is wrong, you will miss the work of God. We can get so focused on what we don't know that we do not create space for God to show up, and as a result, we miss the opportunity to experience signs, wonders, and miracles. Know what you can change and influence but do not allow the adversities at work or in the world to keep you from experiencing a life of joy and keeping your peace. Watch your energy because everyone does not deserve access, and those energy vampires will take and take and take if you do not guard against them. I've made a commitment to myself to laugh more and often. No matter what is going on around me, I can smile knowing that there is something greater within me at work. Rest in knowing that God promises peace. You must be willing to receive it.

SCRIPTURES TO CONSIDER

There is neither Jew nor Greek, there is neither slave nor free man, there is neither male nor female; for you are all one in Christ Jesus. (Galatians 3:28)

For there is no distinction between Jew and Greek; for the same Lord is Lord of all, and is rich to all who call on him. (Romans 10:12)

After these things I looked, and behold, a great multitude, which no man could count, out of every nation and of all tribes, peoples, and languages, standing before the throne and before the Lamb, dressed in white robes, with palm branches in their hands. (Revelation 7:9)

QUESTIONS FOR REFLECTION

1. How have you dealt with racism or sexism in the workplace?
2. What tangible steps can you take to protect yourself from "weathering"?
3. How do you embrace the seasons of your life? Is there an opportunity to create a ritual to celebrate and remember the changes God has brought you through?

PRAYER

Father, help me recognize my blind spots. I recognize that we live in a fallen world that is plagued with the sin of racism and the abuse of power. You created each of us in your image and there is no distinction in your view of us. We are all a part of your royal priesthood and in you, there is no difference. We were called and chosen by you to do the work assigned by you to build your kingdom on earth. Help us to be bridges of love to those we encounter and not to create barriers but remove them so we can all experience your best for our lives. Empower us to be people of light in every space we enter. In Jesus' name, amen.

11

Interviewing, Negotiating, and Getting the Role

ONE OF MY CLIENTS recently shared that she was proud of me because I asked for my worth during contract negotiations. She couldn't tell me what was available in the budget, but she alluded to the fact that I needed to go higher. I remember drafting the proposal for this particular contract and going back and forth about whether I was asking too much. I would counter that question with, "Am I asking for enough and for what I need?"

My accountant reminds me about one of his clients who just throws out the highest number in negotiations to see how others respond. It's worked for him. I'm not that bold, but I do know that asking for what I need and want in negotiating salaries or contracts previously has been a challenge for me, as it is for many women.

According to research by Deepa Purushothaman, Deborah M. Kolb, Hannah Riley Bowles, and Valerie Purdie-Greenaway, many women struggle to negotiate effectively for fair pay and benefits. This chapter discusses strategies for us to advocate for our worth, such as saying no when needed, asking for fair compensation, and not undervaluing ourselves even before applying for a role.

I vividly recall approaching my college graduation, brimming with excitement about not just completing my degree but starting a career and earning a steady income after years of being a broke student. In my eagerness, I accepted the first job offer that came my way, via a friend, without negotiating salary or fully vetting the role. At $12,000 annually for a full-time position in 1992, the pay was paltry. Moreover, my friend was an unreliable character, making it a risky proposition. The opportunity dissolved when I got into a car accident, which delayed the process and proved serendipitous. Another employer called with an offer at more than double the salary! I was stunned by the $25,000 offer at just twenty-one years old, which—keep in mind—was decent for a twenty-one-year-old with limited experience more than thirty years ago. In retrospect, I realize my mistake in not negotiating salary or carefully evaluating fit with that first job offer (the $12K). I let excitement cloud my judgment. This set my salary history artificially low, which impacted me for years after, as employers generally base offers on previous pay. Despite often having more experience and qualifications than colleagues in similar roles, I discovered they made substantially more. The lesson is clear: know your worth in the market, vet job offers thoroughly, negotiate salary and benefits, and remember you are assessing the employer just as they assess you.

Approach the job search as mutually finding the best match, not just desperately grabbing the first offer. Had I learned this sooner, it would have spared me years of underpayment. For those not inclined toward entrepreneurship as I eventually pursued, negotiating is crucial to fair pay.

One of my mentees told me she felt she should be paid based on what the job was worth. I reminded her that certain positions can create more financial opportunity, for instance, a C-suite team member makes more than a person who is entry-level. Yet managers are not paying you solely based on title and role. They are paying for the experience you bring. Many women do not elaborate on their experience or transferable skills from volunteering, going to school, or raising children. You must be your biggest advocate.

KNOW THE BARRIERS

According to a recent Lean In report, Black women face more workplace microaggressions and barriers to advancement than women of other races. They are also more likely to have their skills doubted by colleagues. The report also found that from 2017 to 2021, women leaders of all races quit their jobs at higher rates than men. Reasons included advancement barriers, being overworked without credit, and desiring more flexibility.[1] Company culture and environment have a major impact.

The authors of the article "Negotiating as a Woman of Color" draw from interviews with 1,000 executives and professionals who are women of color to demonstrate how cultural backgrounds and stereotypes affect negotiation abilities.[2] Specifically, they find that many women of color feel discouraged from negotiating, with Black women cautious of being seen as "angry" or "difficult" if they reveal ambition, Asian women taught to revere authority figures, and Latinas advised to avoid "rocking the boat." For these women, overcoming such ingrained beliefs and stereotypes presents an added challenge when asserting their worth.

CODE SWITCHING IN THE WORKPLACE

Many women of color practice code switching, defined as the ability to adapt one's language, dialect, and tone to fit different social contexts with ease.[3] Code switching can even involve withholding personal details that may not be viewed favorably in order to conform to cultural norms.

Code switching is more prevalent among younger Black college graduates, those ages eighteen to forty-nine, than older college-educated Black adults over fifty and Black adults without college degrees in both age groups.[4] Code switching prevents individuals from expressing their authentic selves, and companies miss out when employees cannot be themselves in the workplace.

THE CONFIDENCE GAP

The confidence gap poses another challenge for women of color. Research shows that women tend to underestimate their abilities more than men, despite equal competence. This gap is magnified for women of color, who often feel they must prove their worth in White, male-dominated workplaces. Feeling like the "first" or "only one" at an organization can exacerbate self-doubt. The feeling that you must represent your entire community and overperform to gain acceptance is overwhelming. Stereotype threat—the risk of confirming negative stereotypes about one's racial, ethnic, gender, or cultural group—also erodes confidence, as women of color fear confirming negative assumptions.

Research shows that women are less likely to self-promote than men, even when equally qualified.[5] This tendency stems from a lack of confidence, not ability. It is critical that women own their worth by reflecting on their education, experience, transferable skills, and depth of lived experience.

The intersection of race and gender can make women of color feel they don't belong in corporate spaces dominated by White men.[6] Furthermore, the "glass cliff" phenomenon—being appointed a leadership role in an already struggling organization—deters women of color from pursuing advancement, as failure gets attributed to them personally rather than the circumstances.[7]

I've seen this phenomenon up close. A friend of mine took over as CEO at a large nonprofit that had been previously led by White men. She moved to a new city and was unaware of all the challenges in the organization, including numerous financial difficulties. The men in power before her had chance after chance to fix these problems but did not. After my friend assumed the role and became aware of the organization's dire financial situation, she reached out for support and found very little. She had to make some difficult decisions, and she's not the only one. I've seen numerous nonprofit groups bring in people of color to lead only to have the agencies close, creating a narrative that these leaders were not responsible or competent. There is no mention of the multiple issues these leaders inherited and the lack of support they received in navigating through those challenges. This may seem far-fetched but it happens more than many realize. Leaders in these situations can't allow themselves to be robbed of their confidence and what they know to be true about their abilities and calling.

The key is to build confidence by focusing on one's own unique talents and voice instead of seeking validation through biased corporate norms. With self-assurance and community support, women of color can overcome barriers, fulfill their potential, and bring diverse perspectives to leadership roles. My friend who inherited the financially failing agency has done a great job of tapping into her village for support to endure this difficult and painful transition.

Own your value and acknowledge your skills and experience. Do not let self-doubt hold you back from leadership. With an accurate understanding of your abilities and support to overcome biases, you can achieve your leadership potential.

THE INTERVIEW

During the interview process, it's critical to learn as much as possible about the company's stance on diversity and inclusion. Thoroughly research the company by checking their website, social media, Glassdoor, and LinkedIn. Look for a culture statement, commitments to equity and belonging, responses to recent social issues, and employee reviews. Prepare to ask specific questions about how women of color are treated, promoted, paid, supported, and retained.

Sample questions include:

- What policies support flexible schedules and working parents?
- How many women of color are in senior roles?
- What growth opportunities exist for new hires?

- Is there a diversity department or are there employee resource groups?
- How did leadership respond internally to recent social issues?
- Inquire about pay equity, promotions, caregiver support, and professional development.

Reaching out to current employees can also provide candid insight. Get their perspective on team culture and whether they would recommend the company. Also reach out to current employees from underrepresented groups to get their perspective on feeling supported, professional development, conflict resolution, and retention.[8]

Overall, going into an interview informed and prepared with thoughtful questions will reveal whether the company truly supports and uplifts women of color. The goal is to determine whether the company truly walks the walk when it comes to providing the support you need to be successful.

THE NEGOTIATION PROCESS

One of the biggest mistakes I've made is allowing companies to use my previous pay as base for salary offers. I was always so happy to get a pay bump from what I'd been making in the past that I didn't take into account the expectations, responsibilities, and workload I would be assuming in the new role.

Typically, after you complete a set of interviews and possible assessments, if a company is interested in hiring you, they will perform reference and background checks before extending an offer.

If you have something that might be flagged in a background check, let the hiring manager know what may be discovered. Many jobs do not take applications and only receive résumés, so it's important to let them know proactively. More companies are embracing individuals with backgrounds, but there is still a lot of fear. Do not allow your background or lapses in employment to deter you from applying. It just means that you need to tell your story. You can inform the employer about the Federal Bonding Program, a free program that covers employers for up to six months of employment with coverage amounts starting at $5,000. Visit bonds4jobs.com for more information.

Be careful who you allow to provide a reference for you. When I was working at a nonprofit two decades ago, a friend applied for a role at the agency. One of her references, whom she thought was a friend, gave her a horrible review. My supervisor was not going to hire my friend because of the reference but let her know the situation without disclosing the person's identity. This doesn't usually happen—a lot of people are just discarded from the process without knowing that someone gave a poor reference.

When my friend Debra was applying for a role, she asked me for another friend's contact information for a reference. Debra had met this person briefly a few times, and because she was renowned in our area, Debra thought her name would lend credibility to her application. Ultimately Debra did not receive the recommendation. Debra's not the only person I've experienced this with. I've had individuals I don't know reach out and ask me for a letter of recommendation. It's easy to read a letter and determine if the person has a relationship with the letter writer. Focus on someone who knows your character, skill, and ability and can attest personally to what you can bring to the company.

Once you are selected for the position and receive an offer letter, this is the time to begin negotiating. This can be an intimidating process, but view it as an opportunity to advocate for yourself. Too many of us become fixated on how much we are being paid without exploring flexibility, benefits, career growth, and organizational culture. Before agreeing to a job offer, research the fair market value for the role to inform salary negotiations. Examine industry-specific salary surveys, professional organizations' studies, and trade associations' data to benchmark pay rates based on your skills and experience. Consider regional cost of living differences and median salaries from the Bureau of Labor Statistics. Review pay transparency laws,[9] nonprofit 990 forms through ProPublica, and salary databases. A great resource is Fair360, a database of larger companies that compiles data about gender, race, and other factors.

Studies show women of color often provide dramatically lower minimum salary requirements than White men. One study found that women of color started jobs with minimum salaries 40% less than those of White men, while minimum pay for men of color was 30% lower and minimum salaries for White women were 25% lower than those of White men.[10]

But don't just focus on money in the negotiation process. If employee stock ownership is available, take advantage of it. Research shows that employees with stock ownership in their company earn 30% higher income and accumulate greater household wealth compared to their peers without company stock. Offering a transparent employee stock purchase plan can boost nonsalary compensation for workers.[11]

Also, if you care for a relative or child, inquire about what support the company provides for caregivers. For example, are there mentorship or sponsorship programs to help employees balance work and caregiving responsibilities? Will the company pay for your student loans? Many firms are offering this benefit or even tuition reimbursement. Ask about this, along with opportunities to obtain certifications related to your job.

Know your worth and take the risk to negotiate pay that reflects your value. Recognize that gender and racial biases often lead women and people of color to undervalue ourselves. Have confidence in your worth and negotiate ambitiously. As I tell my daughter, always bet on yourself.

For women of color already in leadership roles who are being assigned additional responsibilities, the authors of *Negotiating as a Woman of Color* suggest using negotiation tactics such as these:[12]

- State that accepting new duties would require dropping other priorities.

- Agree to a new role in exchange for a desired opportunity in the future.
- Decline an immediate yes and ask for time to consider.
- Seek clarity on how the assignment aligns with priorities and performance metrics.
- Propose a trial period before fully committing.
- When appropriate, let strategic silence prompt further explanation.

To negotiate a higher salary in your current role, review industry salary surveys and your company's salary audit, if available. Additionally, consult HR professionals and recruiters to understand how your salary compares to similar positions elsewhere. When you are negotiating, come up with your list of talking points. Make sure you have examples that demonstrate your ability to do the job. This is the time to highlight your past experiences, education, certifications, and accomplishments. Rehearse your talking points with someone who will give you honest feedback. Finally, know that every offer isn't for you—it is okay to walk away from something that does not serve your needs.

Though discrimination and racism persist in workplaces, we must have faith that God has a purpose for each of us. We cannot let others' prejudices and lack of understanding undermine our knowledge that we are precious in God's eyes. A support system is crucial when you are job searching or starting a new role. Surround yourself with people who serve as a mirror, reflecting your inner strengths and talents. Bask in the affirmation of God's perception of us as special and valuable. Internalize this truth deeply. Enter the application, interview, and negotiation process with confidence, knowing your worth in God's eyes.

Reflect on the rejections you've experienced. I once interviewed extensively for a position only to be turned down, which left me quite frustrated. In retrospect, I see that God spared me from an unhealthy work environment, as that organization later collapsed. Rest assured, God has a purposeful plan for you. As Romans 8:28 promises, "All things work together for good for those who love God." Can you recognize God's protective hand guiding you?

BIBLICAL POINT OF VIEW: HANNAH

In 1 Samuel 1–2 we read the story of Hannah, who was married to Elkanah. Hannah was taunted by Elkanah's first wife, Peninnah, for being barren. Every year Hannah would pray for a child, becoming so desperate that the priest, Eli, thought she was drunk as she cried out to God in the temple. Hannah promised God that if she bore a child, she would give that child back to God. God heard her prayers and Hannah conceived. She bore one of the greatest prophets in the Bible, Samuel. In addition to Samuel, Hannah had three other sons and two daughters. God honored her faithfulness.

Hannah teaches us the power of perseverance. She never gave up on herself and she definitely did not give up on God! God has placed a dream in each of us, and we cannot allow the taunts of others and the pressures of the world to stop us from going for what is God's best for us! Can God honor your faithfulness?

SCRIPTURES TO CONSIDER

> For we were saved in hope, but hope that is seen is not hope. For who hopes for that which he sees? But if we hope for that which we don't see, we wait for it with patience. (Romans 8:24-25)

> Let's not be weary in doing good, for we will reap in due season, if we don't give up. So then, as we have opportunity, let's do what is good toward all men, and especially toward those who are of the household of the faith. (Galatians 6:9-10)

> Therefore let's also, seeing we are surrounded by so great a cloud of witnesses, lay aside every weight and the sin which so easily

entangles us, and let's run with perseverance the race that is set before us. (Hebrews 12:1)

QUESTIONS FOR REFLECTION

1. Do you have an elevator speech—a thirty- to sixty-second self-introduction? The goal of an elevator speech is to make an impression so that others want to know more about you. It should highlight your experience and what you can offer and include a call to action: What should people do when they hear your pitch? Visit your website? Email you? Practice your elevator speech so you come across as confident, clear, and engaging.
2. Answer the following questions, which are typical questions interviewers ask job applicants. Practice with a friend:
   - What are your strengths?
   - Why should we hire you?
   - How do you resolve conflict?
   - Where do you see yourself in five years?

PRAYER

Thank you, God, for making me fearfully and wonderfully in your image. I am grateful that my uniqueness is a gift from you and that even before I was born you had a beautiful destiny for me. It brings you joy to bless me, so I seek to align my will with yours. I trust that whatever is meant for me will come, and if something is not, I know you have something better in store. I pray all this in the powerful name of Jesus Christ, amen.

12

The Impact of White Supremacy on Organizational Culture

MANY OF US FAIL TO UNDERSTAND the impact of white supremacy on our lives and the way it exists in organizations. As people of color we can even uphold white supremacy without realizing it. If we take time to understand its characteristics, we can enact racial equity principles to counter its impact.

We often equate white supremacy with notorious hate groups such as the Ku Klux Klan. However, it often manifests in more subtle ways: Whiteness has long been centered in society, from America to the world at large. This centering does not inherently make White people bad, but it harms everyone by upholding unjust racial hierarchies. People of color face direct oppression, while White people lose their full humanity under a flawed system. As Christians, we believe God cherishes all people equally. To live out God's vision, we must replace white supremacy with a centering of God's universal love.

> Know therefore that those who are of faith are children of Abraham. The Scripture, foreseeing that God would justify the Gentiles by faith, preached the Good News beforehand to Abraham, saying, "In you all the nations will be blessed." So then, those who are of faith are blessed with the faithful Abraham. . . .

For you are all children of God, through faith in Christ Jesus. For as many of you as were baptized into Christ have put on Christ. There is neither Jew nor Greek, there is neither slave nor free man, there is neither male nor female; for you are all one in Christ Jesus. If you are Christ's, then you are Abraham's offspring and heirs according to promise. (Galatians 3:7-9, 26-29)

Organizations committed to rectifying racial inequality must move beyond diversity and inclusion programs toward reparations and restitution. Most companies fail to recognize how their systems and processes negatively impact employees. Just as a house requires a solid foundation, organizations should ensure their core values and culture foster equity, not uphold biases, however unintentional. Until systemic injustices are acknowledged and repaired at the root, progress stalls. Diversity efforts driven by politics rather than ethics inevitably backfire. True inclusion means creating spaces where everyone feels safe and valued for who they are.

HOW WHITENESS SHOWS UP

Whiteness can show up in society in various ways, often reflecting historical and systemic power dynamics. Let's take a look at some of the most common.

Privilege. The word *privilege* has been demonized in our society, but the reality is that certain identities have opportunities that others do not. For instance, laws were created in this country's inception that favored White men, especially those in positions of power or with wealth. This allowed men to become property owners and vote. Women fought for suffrage in the early 1900s, and communities of color were not allowed to vote until after civil rights legislation was enacted. Women and people of color have been historically disadvantaged because of their lack of access to resources such as homeownership, voting, and leadership opportunities.

It's important to note that privilege does not just show up in race and gender. I recognize that even as a Black woman, two marginalized identities, I also have access to opportunities as a result of being a PhD and a business owner. Other privileges come with being Christian, heterosexual, and able-bodied—the spaces I am in often cater to these identities. As women of color we must own the complexities of our identities and not allow society to value one more than the other.

Absence of representation. When I visited India, I marveled at the number of billboards featuring White, blue-eyed, blond-haired individuals towering over a sea of Brown people. In the stores I was shocked by the number of skin bleaching and hair dye products available. When I asked about this, I was told that many Indian people grayed young, and because black hair dye was not readily available, colors like red and strawberry blond were used. Individuals classed as the Dalits, or untouchables, were often darker-complected, and that wasn't something non-Dalits wanted to be associated with. It saddened me to see that a country filled with Brown people did not have representation in their culture highlighting and amplifying who they are.

As a child, I watched television shows such as *Good Times* and *The Jeffersons* because I wanted to see people who looked like me. I had few options. *Good Times* bothered me, because despite the family's many talents, they never had the opportunity to leave the projects. Some obstacle always prevented them from getting out. The messaging was not the best. At least with *The Jeffersons*, I could envision what Black wealth could be like.

Representation matters. When people of color are not included in media, politics, or other influential platforms, our experiences are not shared and our communities are perceived as monolithic when they are anything but. It's important to be at the table. If we are not, we need to create our own rooms and buildings.

Cultural appropriation. Cultural appropriation is taking the culture of another group without giving credit to that group and using it outside its original intent. There is a difference between appreciation and appropriation. Appreciation respects different cultural elements without exploiting or profiting from the work of others. Appropriation perpetuates stereotypes and denies narratives and context from being shared by those with the lived experience.

Jazz was extremely popular in Louisiana when I was a child. Jazz originated in ragtime and blues, two major Black musical genres, and was a part of New Orleans culture. These musical customs and the impact of Black music on rock-and-roll are both part of American history. Elvis Presley referred to renowned blues guitarist Fats Domino as the "real king of rock-and-roll." Domino claimed that in the 1960s, the music he had been performing in New Orleans for more than ten years was being referred to as rock-and-roll.[1] Compared to their White peers, the majority of these Black musicians had limited success in the music industry or credit for their accomplishments.

Appropriation takes place in fashion as well. In fact, it's so common that the Mexican Senate in 2021 passed legislation prohibiting the cultural appropriation of Indigenous and Afro-Mexican artists' works. Through the decades this cultural history has been preserved through crafts, needlework, and other artistic endeavors. The purpose of intellectual property legislation is to safeguard these groups' creative output so that others cannot control or profit from it when they steal it.[2] Asian cultures also experience cultural appropriation in regard to food and dress.

Cultural interactions are acceptable. But instead of making money off the creators and telling a new story without them, it's critical that we respect and pay tribute to them. As women of color, how do we own and embrace our history and the elements of our culture?

Colorism. Colorism is the discriminatory practice of giving preference to an individual with lighter skin tone over one with a darker complexion. Colorism is not exclusive to America; it is also present in India, Mexico, and Southeast Asia, among other countries.[3] Skin color has been a point of contention among African Americans with a history dating back to slavery, when lighter Blacks were allowed to work in the house instead of the field.

When I was growing up, I was conflicted about skin tone. My mother, who was very light as a child, was picked on and did not see lighter skin as an advantage. As a result, color was not an issue in my household, and I enjoyed basking in the sunlight. If anything, being darker was celebrated. My father was dark-skinned. Yet at school, lighter girls were the ones considered pretty. It was frowned on to play outside for long periods of time because of the possibility of getting darker.

Being light-skinned provides several benefits in terms of partner selection, education, money, and lifestyle, according to one researcher.[4] Many of us have adopted this way of thinking and behaving unwittingly; White beauty is so prevalent in the media that it has conditioned us to feel it is the standard. Racism and colorism are real, and they show up in our interactions with both our own communities and the dominant culture. Investigating how colorism is present in the workplace is crucial. What does it mean for us as leaders to examine our attitudes in this area? How does colorism manifest itself in our relationships? What messages are we giving regarding color?

Institutional racism. Many people believe racism is easy to spot. But racism isn't just the use of derogatory speech or actively denying a person housing or a job because of their skin color. Institutional racism is embedded in many of the systems and structures we participate in daily. It includes doctors believing Black people can tolerate more pain than other groups. It shows up when women of color receive subpar medical care. One study found that breast and cervical cancer claim more lives of Latinas than non-Latina women,[5] and the Centers for Disease Control and Prevention report the maternal mortality rate for Black women at about seventy deaths per 100,000 live births—2.6 times the rate for non-Latino White women.[6] Serena Williams's story shows that wealth and status do not prevent a Black woman from the possibility of dying in childbirth.[7] These factors demonstrate a system plagued with issues affecting women of color.

Racism can be embedded in laws and policies as well. For instance, Black and Latino men's sentences are 13.4% and 11.2% longer, respectively, than White males' sentences for the same crimes.[8] Compared to White females, Black and Latina females are less likely to be placed on probation (11.2% and 29.7%, respectively).[9] These trends affect families and often have generational consequences. As women of color in leadership, how can we pay attention to these systems and how they impact our lives and the lives of those around us? How can we identify workplace policies that are unfair to employees of color, clients, or community members, then address them?

CHARACTERISTICS OF WHITE SUPREMACY

We are all impacted and shaped by white supremacy whether we are conscious of it or not. The more insidious characteristics of white supremacy steer us toward harmful behaviors that serve no one, even in the absence of the overt violence we usually associate with this subject. Tema Okun, writing on the White Supremacy Culture website, presents a number of traits that are overrepresented in white supremacy culture and tend to be self-perpetuating through its institutions and standards. We need to be aware of these characteristics, especially in terms of how they harm our workplaces:[10]

Perfectionism. Perfectionism is the urge to ensure that everything is completely flawless. We exhaust ourselves in an effort to get things precisely right. This does not benefit us, because the only perfect entity is God and God's plan (see Psalm 18:30).

Sense of urgency. When there is a constant feeling of being rushed, everything seems like an emergency. This mindset doesn't acknowledge that people process and react at different speeds. It causes anxiety, and the Bible tells us to give our worries to God (1 Peter 5:7).

When we are always in a hurry, we are attempting to take control. We don't leave room for God or time for reflection and renewal.

It's also important that we begin to prioritize rest. God did not call us to a life of striving. Work is important to God but not at the expense of our health and well-being. When I was younger, I felt like I was on a hamster wheel of making things happen. Those unnamed voices of "they and them" control so much of the self-imposed timelines we live by. We feel that at a certain age we must accomplish various goals. We feel we need to be married, with kids, or have purchased a home by a certain age. This way of thinking keeps us from including God in our plans and enjoying the process. It also robs us of our peace and rest because we are always in a hurry, too busy to take the time to enjoy our lives because of the invisible clock we find ourselves adhering to. As leaders, we must begin to focus not just on mantras that state rest is important but begin to operationalize what this looks like in our policies and procedures.

Defensiveness. This behavior stems from a desire to shield ourselves and our self-image from any negative judgment. It is grounded in a fear of having our flaws revealed. When we are in this mindset, deflection comes more naturally than direct confrontation of problems. For many groups, questioning power or accepted norms feels too risky. There is a preference for upholding traditional methods without considering new options because of what we might need to sacrifice in the process.

More is better. Nonprofit leaders understand all too well the mandate to serve more people and scale the work rather than going deeper to ensure that transformation is truly occurring. Funders drive organizations to do more with limited resources, and board members agree—without seeking to understand the challenges leaders are facing—because they are driven by the possibility of increased visibility and funding. This compromises the integrity of the work and the sustainability of the organization. A focus on quantity over quality does not lead to meaningful progress or social change. Nonprofits should be cautious about growth for growth's sake and stay true to their purpose, even if that means maintaining a smaller scale of operations.

Elevation of the written word. Many communities of color have grown out of a rich and beautiful oral tradition. But white supremacy culture values the written word above verbal communication. When we place more value on emails than face-to-face conversations, we are missing opportunities to connect deeply. In today's climate of misinformation and "fake news," it's important to remember that not everything committed to writing represents absolute truth or the best ideals.

Paternalism. Paternalism manifests in the workplace when leaders presume they understand what is ideal for their staff. I witness this often in community development. Organizations and churches often enter communities of color thinking they have the solutions rather than listening to the people most impacted—those who understand their own needs better than anyone else. Paternalism shows up in decision-making that does not allow others to co-create solutions for their wants and needs. It is a form of exerting control. Years ago I had a supervisor who would go to my colleague's office next door to mine to eavesdrop on my conversations with students to find out what we were discussing. I learned of this when several students commented on seeing this happen. Paternalism is rooted in a lack of trust and is evident in organizations where communication is limited and flows only from the top down.

Either-or thinking. I frequently advise my daughter that thinking in absolute, binary terms is restrictive. This style of thinking does not allow for different perspectives to coexist simultaneously. In many cases, the answer is not "either-or" but "both/and." When we insist that there is a single correct approach, we overlook fresh ways of conceptualizing issues that could enhance our methods and reveal our biases. By embracing rigid dichotomies, we miss opportunities to evolve our thinking in ways that make us more effective and insightful.

Power hoarding. Holding on to information and not sharing it with others is a form of hoarding power. When only one person has access to key information, it can create problems for an organization. Leaders who hoard information also tend to micromanage their employees. These controlling managers who are insecure about their position stifle creativity and innovation in the workplace. They closely oversee all work because of their need to monitor and direct everything that happens.

Creating fear. Fear is a tactic that is used as a form of control, as when political advertising is used to instill panic. During the 1988 election, George H. W. Bush issued a commercial that featured Willie Horton, a Black man who was on a furlough release program after raping a White woman and stabbing her boyfriend. Bush criticized his opponent, Mike Dukakis, for allowing Horton's release. This focus on race during an election campaign created enormous fear and a dialogue about tougher crime laws that still have an impact today.[11]

Individualism. Many communities of color are very communal and collective. Our families live together with several generations in one household. This lifestyle is counter to the idea of "rugged individualism," a phrase coined by President Hoover to mean that people should not need assistance or support but rely only on themselves.[12] I've heard most of my life about pulling yourself up by your bootstraps. The reality is that most of us need some type of help along the way. The early church demonstrated what it meant to be there for one another (Acts 4:34), and as Christians we are instructed to fellowship with one another (Hebrews 10:24-25). There must be a balance between individual effort and understanding the value and role of the collective.

Objectivity. Objectivity does not take into account that all of us are shaped by our experiences. It is hard to be objective when we bring our historical, cultural, and social experiences to frame the way we see the world. This can show up in invalidating the emotions of others and valuing the rational and logical as better.

Right to comfort. Recently I was creating a presentation for a client, and the team member I was working with expressed concern that my content might offend the client. I wasn't clear on how facts would be offensive. Yet I've witnessed over and over how women of color avoid the challenges brought about by conversations about race and focus on others' comfort over the truth. My goal has never been to intentionally make someone uncomfortable, but if telling the truth hurts, we need to address why. It is unfair for women of color to experience discomfort daily only to ensure that others, especially those in positions of power, are comfortable and free from pain.

These characteristics do not serve us well. What would it look like for us to reimagine the possibilities in our workplaces using the Word of God as a guide to create spaces that honor others? Instead of hoarding power and resources, let's recognize that we do not have to diminish the light of others for ours to shine brighter.

ACTIVATING ALLIES

I think of an ally as someone who stands on the sidelines and cheers for me. Allies use their privilege and platforms to amplify the voices of women of color without co-opting our narratives. They don't speak on behalf of women of color but create and advocate for space for women of color. Allies are important, but I want them to be co-conspirators. I want individuals who are willing to get dirty with me as we navigate these challenging spaces and learn together.

I'll never forget Joni, a young White lady I mentored who said to me, "Froswa', you always talk about having a seat at these tables. What table do you want to sit at? Tell me and I'll help you."

I told her there were tables I was unaware of, and I needed her to speak my name behind closed doors, advocate for me, and create space for me to sit in those rooms. I needed her to speak up when things were said that were offensive and derogatory. One of my friends, the Rev. Mike Baughman, previous executive director and founding pastor of Union Coffee, has always said that people of color did not create racism and should not be expected to end it.

As a woman of color, it's imperative that you identify your allies, cheerleaders, and co-conspirators in your workplace. How can you engage your allies to assist you?

KNOWING WHEN TO PRESERVE YOURSELF

There are times when walking away is necessary for your sanity and safety. Lesley Lokko, the former dean of architecture at the City University of New York who resigned after nine months, stated in a letter that she had to resign in order to preserve her well-being after encountering significant racism in the role.[13] Likewise, Dr. Claudine Gay's resignation from Harvard brought to light the tremendous racism she faced through emails and phone calls.[14]

Toxic workplaces are a reality. Two of my professors at Antioch University, Mitchell Kusy and Elizabeth Holloway, wrote the book *Toxic Workplace! Managing Toxic Personalities and Their Systems of Power.* In it they share how toxic leaders create toxic organizations, referring to toxic leadership as an iceberg with much more below the surface than what we see exposed.[15] I have found in my experience that most toxic leaders are insecure and have a need to control and use methods such as shaming, passive hostility, and sabotage.

We must accept that things will go on without us if we choose to take care of ourselves. As women, we have contributed extensively to our homes, companies, and communities. Facing toxicity on top of these contributions creates stress that takes a toll on our physical, mental, and emotional health. If we are going to help others, we must make sure we take care of ourselves.

BUILDING A VIBRANT AND VIABLE CULTURE AS A LEADER

An organization that is welcoming and allows everyone to experience a sense of belonging must have a culture that promotes this outcome. Leaders must understand and actively manage organizational culture to create a positive work environment, foster employee engagement, and reach key performance indicators. This requires ongoing effort, open communication, and a commitment to continuous improvement.

While a positive and inclusive culture fosters collaboration, innovation, and high performance, a toxic or dysfunctional culture leads to low morale, conflict, and inefficiency. Culture plays a crucial role in shaping communication and collaboration, and leaders play a critical role in shaping and influencing organizational culture. Leaders' behavior, values, and actions set the tone and serve as role models for employees. Effective leaders actively promote and reinforce the desired culture through their decisions, communication, and behaviors.

What are the leaders shaping at your organization? What culture are you contributing to or creating?

SCRIPTURES TO CONSIDER

> Learn to do well.
> Seek justice.
> Relieve the oppressed.
> Defend the fatherless.
> Plead for the widow. (Isaiah 1:17)

> He has shown you, O man, what is good.
> What does Yahweh require of you, but to act justly,
> to love mercy, and to walk humbly with your God? (Micah 6:8)

QUESTIONS FOR REFLECTION

1. How have you experienced the characteristics of white supremacy or Whiteness being centered in the workplace? How have you dealt with it?
2. Have you ever been in a toxic workplace? What did you do to take care of yourself? How did it affect you and the way you see yourself or view work?
3. Who are your allies or co-conspirators? What does it look like to leverage those relationships?

PRAYER

Dear God, our diversity is a source of strength. As women of color, we endure many hardships in our homes, families, workplaces, and communities, which can feel exhausting and overwhelming. Despite the burdens we carry, we know we can find rest in you, for you have said your yoke is easy. Please help us avoid attachments that would steer us from your will. Grant us the wisdom you promise to give freely when asked. We need your guidance and discernment to understand the seasons and spaces of our lives. Thank you for seeing and advocating for us. In Jesus' name we pray, amen.

13

The Case for Diversity, Equity, Inclusion, and Belonging

DIVERSITY, EQUITY, AND INCLUSION (DEI) efforts are not for the faint of heart. Many initiatives have been launched to try to change the hearts of those in the workplace, but they have failed to convey the financial and social implications of this work. In order for diversity initiatives to bring about change, there must be buy-in and the courage to fail forward.

I mentored a young woman in a DEI role who faced significant challenges not only because of her age but because her institution was mired in a system of doing things a certain way. The CEO who hired her was instrumental in making sure she was supported, which is key for large-scale initiatives to work. But she realized she also needed to build allies internally with all levels of staff. Her success in making these efforts a part of the entire organization was tied to relationship building, trust, creating safe spaces, and sharing the vision of what a diverse workplace could do to transform the organization and the community. This young lady was extremely courageous in taking on a new role, recognizing the need for listening, and not creating strategy in isolation.

One of the biblical figures I look to for courageous leadership is Deborah, whose story is found in Judges 4–5. Harvard Business School

Professor Nancy Koehn describes a courageous leader as someone who sees an opportunity for growth during times of crisis and hardship and strengthens their followers' resolve despite the difficult circumstances. Deborah embodies just such qualities. Many women of color are called into leadership roles in the workplace to address challenges related to gender and race, and often we work alone or with just a few co-laborers. Deborah sets an example of how to use our voice even when organizations fail to stand up for who we are.

Deborah is the only female judge in the Old Testament and the only woman to serve both as prophet and judge in Israel's history. Along with Moses and Samuel, she is one of just three figures who held this dual role. Deborah helped deliver Israel from its enemies through her faithfulness to God, partnership with fellow courageous woman Jael, and wise use of her gifts, securing forty years of peace for Israel. Though living in a male-dominated society, Deborah stood firm and made a profound impact.

In the previous chapter, we discussed how white supremacy culture plays out in organizational settings and highlighted the critical need for liberation and equity. After the death of George Floyd at the hands of police on May 5, 2020, many companies released statements, made public pledges, and ultimately established DEI departments—all aiming to confront long-standing inequities in their workplaces.[1] Many of us as women of color were appointed to positions of responsibility for this work in addition to our existing roles. We were tasked with examining whether not just equality and equity but also liberation could exist in White-led organizations.

According to LinkedIn data, chief diversity and inclusion officer postings saw a surge of nearly 170% starting in 2020, with related roles such as chief people officer also rising sharply.[2] However, many of these new positions lacked adequate budget, staffing, and direction. As a result, turnover has been high and some roles have been eliminated entirely due to unrealistic expectations, insufficient support, and companies' desire for quick results. Despite bold pledges, many companies have yet to fulfill substantial financial commitments to these efforts and some, such as Tractor Supply Company in June 2024, have eliminated DEI departments completely.[3]

Just Capital's corporate racial equity database tracks and analyzes diversity and pay equity data disclosed by companies. In 2021 and 2022, the database showed significant increases in companies reporting workforce and board diversity statistics, as well as racial and ethnic pay equity analyses—areas where investors have applied growing pressure. Specifically, workforce diversity disclosure rose 6% from 86% to 91%, board diversity disclosure grew 13% from 84% to 95%, racial/ethnic pay equity analysis disclosure jumped 33% from 34% to 45%, and disclosure of racial/ethnic pay ratios increased 71% from 14% to 24%.[4]

Still, Just Capital also found that corporate America continues to lag on key social issues. For example, only 7% of 100 leading companies disclosed internal promotion rates by race/ethnicity in 2022. Just 9% reported local small business spending amounts. Only 11% had reentry or second chance hiring policies. A mere 14% reported funding for local public schools. Just 21% conducted anti-harassment training, despite 98% having anti-harassment policies. Only 22% disclosed actual pay equity analysis results by race. Just 23% set diversity hiring, promotion, or retention targets by race. Only 36% had anti-forced labor policies for suppliers, with a mere 14% implementing this policy internally. In summary, the study revealed that most major corporations fail to fully disclose or act on critical social justice and equity issues.[5]

In addition to pledging systemic changes within their organizations, many companies also pledged financial contributions to promote racial equity. McKinsey and Company has tracked these corporate efforts since 2020, finding that between May 2021 and October 2022, eighty companies, or 8% of all companies surveyed, pledged an additional $141 billion.[6] This compares to 18% of companies pledging funds from May to November 2020, and 10% pledging funds from November 2020 to May 2021. While the total dollar amounts pledged have cumulatively grown, reflecting ongoing corporate commitments to support racial equity, the year-over-year pace of new monetary pledges has slowed by 32% since 2021. Although financial companies accounted for most of the pledged money, they have some of the lowest numbers of Black employees among all industries surveyed.[7]

In addition, terms like *intersectionality* have become politicized and efforts to dismantle DEI departments have grown in recent years, especially in higher education. On May 15, 2023, Florida became the first state to sign a law prohibiting DEI spending at public colleges.[8] In January 2024, Texas enacted a law eliminating DEI programs and promoting a merit-based approach, implying that diverse college applicants are unqualified and taking spots from others.[9] Under the law, Texas public colleges cannot create diversity offices, hire DEI staff, or mandate DEI training for jobs or admission. Policies must be gender- and color-blind. However, as discussed previously, history shows that such "blindness" has been problematic in the United States.

FROM DEI TO BELONGING

As the conversation around racial equity continues to evolve, more organizations are moving away from diversity initiatives and embracing concepts like belonging and targeted universalism. The Institute of Belonging and Othering has done extensive research showing the value of targeted universalism over traditional diversity programs. Targeted universalism sets universal goals for all groups, then implements targeted strategies to help each group achieve those goals based on their specific needs and situations.[10] This approach maintains a shared end goal while allowing for tailored processes. As organizations question the effectiveness of their diversity efforts, I've encouraged them to explore targeted universalism as an alternative way to address systemic inequities that still uplifts everyone.

Belonging in the workplace means employees can bring their authentic selves to work without feeling pressured to adopt a different persona. Fostering a sense of belonging has become a top priority for organizations today. Deloitte's 2020 Human Capital Trends report ranked belonging as the number one human capital issue facing companies.[11] What's more, studies show that belonging benefits the bottom line. According to *Harvard Business Review*, high belonging led to a 56% increase in job performance, a 50% decrease in turnover risk, and a 75% drop in sick days.[12] Clearly, belonging is critical for organizational success.

As diversity continues to be vilified, organizations must actively embrace inclusion and belonging. Targeted universalism and a focus on belonging can serve as useful tools to further this conversation. However, it is critical that we move beyond moral arguments when advocating for inclusive policies and practices. Organizations that intentionally cultivate diversity experience many benefits:

- They gain a deeper understanding of the communities they serve.
- They become more innovative and make better decisions.
- They outperform nondiverse peers.
- Employees experience greater job satisfaction, trust, and engagement.

Keep in mind that transforming organizational culture takes time. Conducting equity audits can uncover overlooked areas for improvement as we build inclusion and belonging.

PRACTICES TO CONSIDER

Harvard Business Review recommends gathering, tracking, and benchmarking data as a way to promote diversity.[13] Specifically, the authors advise companies to collect diversity metrics over time, compare them against other organizations, and share the findings with stakeholders. Doing so can boost accountability and transparency around diversity efforts. To enable this shift, leaders must change their mindset to view complaints not as threats but as valuable insights that can catalyze positive organizational change. Companies should proactively assess new technologies and policies for potential discriminatory impacts on employees before deployment, as well as conduct ongoing audits of implemented systems to detect any emerging biases. When individuals belong to groups underrepresented in the workplace, stereotyping or tokenism can happen. These biases then negatively impact workers and organizations, hindering progress. It's important to be aware of tokenism and how this shows up in the workplace.

Here are some questions to ask as you evaluate practices and policies in your workplace:

- How do the identities of those on staff and in leadership reflect the community?
- How are decisions made in your organization? Who makes decisions? Who is included? Who isn't and why?
- How do you evaluate policies? Who is involved in reviewing those policies? Are there policies that are harmful to marginalized populations?
- How do you include community representation and voice in your organization's operations?

It's also critical to examine the following to ensure accountability and transparency in these efforts:

- Board leadership
- Senior leadership—talent development and succession planning
- Staffing—talent development and succession planning
- Volunteers
- Partnerships, vendors, suppliers
- Customers, clients, congregants
- Programming
- Marketing, branding, PR, communications

CALLING IT OUT

I know a Black woman who heads an affiliate model of a national organization. Three of her direct reports are White women. The team has had some challenges dealing with microaggressions in the workplace. They have worked consistently to call out those actions and statements when they've happened, and it's been wonderful to watch the Black leader call out bad behavior but maintain a spirit of love. In addition, one of the White women takes responsibility for her words and actions and is willing to hold others accountable when they are out of order.

Creating the change we'd like to see in the workplace doesn't happen immediately. Change can begin with something as small as tracking the experiences of women of color within an organization. It's also important to build a diverse and supportive network in the organization—advocates and allies are important. Consider a racial equity audit as a first step to developing strategies to address lack of diversity in the organization. This is a great tool to use to evaluate every facet of the organization as you begin to make changes. Are there opportunities to either join or create an affinity group that brings various identities together to solve issues in your workplace?

When making efforts to improve your organization, be mindful of potential obstacles that can hinder success: long-standing organizational problems and leaders who are not fully committed. Nonparticipation by staff and departmental silos can also impede these attempts to shift organizational culture. Tackling these challenges early on will help your efforts be more successful.

For those working in these spaces, it is crucial to establish regular self-care rituals—and I don't just mean massages, facials, or pedicures. While pampering treats are enjoyable, true self-care means committing to practices that nourish you consistently, not just when you feel overwhelmed.

SCRIPTURES TO CONSIDER

After these things I looked, and behold, a great multitude, which no man could count, out of every nation and of all tribes, peoples, and languages, standing before the throne and before the Lamb, dressed in white robes, with palm branches in their hands. They cried with a loud voice, saying, "Salvation be to our God, who sits on the throne, and to the Lamb!" (Revelation 7:9-10)

For by him all things were created in the heavens and on the earth, visible things and invisible things, whether thrones or dominions or principalities or powers. All things have been created through him and for him. He is before all things, and in him all things are held together. (Colossians 1:16-17)

Be of the same mind one toward another. Don't set your mind on high things, but associate with the humble. Don't be wise in your own conceits. (Romans 12:16)

Be strong and courageous; for you shall cause this people to inherit the land which I swore to their fathers to give them. (Joshua 1:6)

QUESTIONS FOR REFLECTION

1. How does your company approach diversity and inclusion efforts?
2. Do you feel a sense of belonging at work? What factors make you feel this way?
3. How does Joshua 1:6 apply to you in the workplace?

PRAYER

Dear God, I lift up every woman who has felt unseen, unvalued, or silenced. Heal her heart from the pain of being minimized. Help her see her true worth as you see it, not through the flawed perspectives of others. Do not let bitterness or indifference take root. Remind her that her value is not dependent on outside approval, for she was cherished since the day she was born.

Strengthen every woman who has lost her fight, her boldness, her voice amid uphill battles. Fill her with your joy, peace, and courage to persist. Let her rise up undaunted by difficulties, walking by faith. Assure her that you alone determine her potential and purpose, not earthly limitations. Part the waters; move mountains on her behalf. Let no one deny her worth or stifle her growth.

Sustain those advocating for women's equality. When they grow weary, renew their passion for justice. Grant them wisdom to soften hardened minds and challenge unconscious bias. Help create a culture that celebrates the gifts of all women.

Remind every woman that she is treasured not just for a day, but every day. In the precious name of Jesus, amen.[14]

14

Coaching Up, Power Dynamics, and Change Management

COACHING UP IS NOT SOMETHING you can tell your supervisor you are doing. It involves addressing areas where your boss may have limitations. Whether these deficits are blind spots or simple arrogance, recognize that there will be times in the workplace when you have to coach your employer.

One of my former staff members used to say she felt sorry for me. In her encounters with my boss, she saw that he was not able to pour into me and wasn't interested in growing me. On top of that, he didn't understand my job and had limited interest in being involved. I was frustrated, because no matter how hard I tried to make it known that I had other skill sets, my boss could only focus on a few aspects of my role. Often I had to intervene to explain the potential damage of certain situations because his experience in my realm of work was almost nonexistent. Even when others would share my abilities with him, it went in one ear and out the other.

I could have easily just gone with the flow, but the consequences would have impacted my work and, ultimately, my peace. So I became astute at building collaborations with other team members to help advocate for causes that were important to me. I also learned how to frame things in a way that helped my boss understand the implications of various decisions.

Coaching up is not about doing someone else's job; it's trying to make your job easier and smoother. If you are young in your leadership journey, it can be stunning to discover that your boss is not as talented or invested as you are. For those of us in spaces that touch people and communities, it's always about centering the community. Bosses will have limitations, but you cannot use that as an excuse to shy away from walking into your potential and purpose. Proverbs 18:16 reminds us that our gifts will make room for us. God could be using this situation with a limited boss to grow you and your leadership.

Abigail is an example in the Bible of what coaching up looks like when we are dealing with someone who is not self-aware or emotionally intelligent. We meet Abigail in 1 Samuel 25 and learn that she was a beautiful and intelligent woman. Her husband, Nabel, who could be called many colorful and inappropriate names, was a wealthy but evil man, and he failed to recognize David or his anointing by God. His refusal to provide assistance for David's troops incensed David, who prepared to slaughter him. If it hadn't been for Abigail's quick thinking, the outcome would have been very different. She decided to bring food to David without telling Nabal and apologized for his stupidity. She recognized who her husband was and, in spite of his foolishness, she was responsible for saving his life.

Abigail is an example to me of what happens when you must coach up. Sometimes we have loved ones or even supervisors we must assist in order to make sure we are given the space to do what we need to do. Coaching up can help your leader, but it also can serve as a way to help save yourself from constant frustration when you are dealing with challenging individuals.

HOW TO COACH UP

Coaching up requires trust. It's important to understand not just the goals of your organization but also those of your leader. Establish a strong relationship with your boss based on respect and open communication, if possible. Like Abigail, assess the situation. Will your boss be receptive to your attempts to help and offer feedback in a constructive and supportive way? Abigail was not able to openly establish a mutually beneficial relationship with her husband, but is this a possibility for you with your supervisor? As a leader, are you creating space to learn from your colleagues and team?

Nabel's name meant "fool," and he exhibited it in many ways. He is a lesson for what we should not do as leaders. He had a brilliant wife and he failed to seek her input and feedback. He was obviously not trustworthy, because she didn't tell him what she was going to do. Nabel was not a proactive problem solver. Instead of trying to collaborate with David, he created a greater problem. He also failed to show empathy and understanding. Just showing David compassion in his time of need could have made a huge difference. How can these lessons from Nabel serve as a guide for your leadership as well as coaching others who may be in authority in your organization or company?

POWER DYNAMICS

Abigail understood the power dynamic that existed between her husband and David. Power dynamics are around us whether we realize it or not. There is a power dynamic between parents and children, spouses, and employees and employers. Power is about the ability to influence or control. In each of the aforementioned relationships, there can be times when one is trying to influence the other to get a need met.

When I was a girl, I asked my mother for a piece of gum. She told me I couldn't have any, and instead of obeying her, I asked my dad. My mother saw me chewing the gum and immediately shared with my dad what she had told me. In my limited six-year-old mind, I did not realize that I was going to be in trouble with both of them. This was an example of a power dynamic. I thought I could outsmart my mother, and it didn't work out well for me! At some point, we all want our way. The problem arises when our way isn't considerate of others and could be harmful.

Power dynamics also come with power imbalances. Abigail lived during a time when women did not have the same rights as men. Men had control over women's existence, and women had to be careful about what they wore, who they spoke to, and what daily activities they participated in. Power imbalances can lead to disparities in our homes and also in our workplaces.

Nabel is someone who abused his power. David needed help, and with his wealth and resources Nabel had the power not to assist him. Abuse of power runs rampant in many of our organizations when individuals are bullied, harassed, or discriminated against.

It's important for us to recognize the way power is used in our organizations. If we are going to have inclusive environments, we can't allow power struggles to become normal. Without open communication, shared decision-making, transparency, accountability, and fairness, organizations and individuals will suffer and not reach their potential.

CHANGE MANAGEMENT AS A TOOL

We often view change management as something only organizations deal with, but we all have to manage change in our lives. Change is something we can expect. It's how we deal with it that makes the difference. For many of us, change happens not because we want it to but because we are forced to change.

In organizations, it's easy to become disgruntled by those who don't understand the vision. But disagreement is an opportunity to ask different questions, lean in, and understand people on a deeper level. After all, people dealing with change are often experiencing loss. Just as there is a grief cycle, there is also a cycle in adjusting to change. The Kübler-Ross curve model states that individuals start in shock and cycle through denial, frustration, depression, experimentation, decision, and integration.[1] We need to recognize that everyone goes through their own process to accept change, and we can allow people the space necessary to adjust.

When we are coaching up or working with our colleagues and employees, our goal is often to create change. But change management is not easy. Kegan and Lahey elaborate on the challenges many of us face when we seek to create change. Typically, people have an "immunity to change"—a cognitive block that prevents us from doing something different.[2] By identifying the cognitive dissonance of these competing commitments (we want to change but something is keeping us from embracing it) and understanding those things that worry us about the change, we can slowly begin to address the barriers that keep us from making the progress we want to see. We can recognize this process in ourselves as well as in those we work with.

Kegan and Lahey also discuss how we make meaning of information and how we all interpret things differently due to our different mindsets. When we try to apply a technical solution to an adaptive challenge (which is what most of our issues are), we come up short and our solutions don't make a difference.[3] True changes require us to do something differently in our behavior, in our thinking, and in our loyalties. This is an adaptive challenge—one that requires change at a deeper level than we realize. Leaders must understand this, because change is inevitable and we won't move ahead if we don't understand what's at stake for people.

A wonderful roadmap for dealing with change is the life of Esther in the Bible. Esther lost both of her parents and was raised by her cousin, Mordecai, who adopted her. She lived during a time when the Israelites had been taken from Jerusalem into captivity in Babylon and other kingdoms. In a different land, she had to learn to adjust.

Ahasuerus, the king of Persia, was seeking a new queen, and Esther was among those being considered by the royal palace. The eunuch Hegai, who was overseeing the preparation of these young women, took a special interest in Esther, providing beauty treatments, additional maids, and special meals. Esther did not reveal her background as a Jewish woman because Mordecai had told her to keep it a secret. The Bible says Esther was beautiful in face and form. She had favor from many in the kingdom. Ultimately, the king fell in love with her.

Once she was queen, Esther had a difficult decision to make. The evil Haman was plotting to have Jews killed throughout the kingdom. Mordecai informed Esther of this and shared that her position as queen was not a coincidence—in fact, she was meant to be in this role for this very moment. Esther went to the king, knowing it was a very risky move that could cost her life. Her decision to face death to save her people demonstrated her character and bravery.

While our physical lives may not be on the line, many of us share similarities with Esther's situation. We are often in environments where we have to mask who we are and we can only reveal pieces of ourselves to others. Esther's life reveals several lessons we can learn from as we deal with change:

- Esther went against the culture at the time. Women did not have much of a voice, and she could have allowed her fear to paralyze her from making a decision. Esther was willing to take a risk. Change often requires us to risk something.
- Mordecai was not just a relative but served as wise counsel for Esther. Before making a difficult decision, Esther sought wisdom and guidance from her uncle. As we face difficult decisions, it's important to consult with those who we trust.
- Building a tribe is important. Esther's relationship with the eunuch Hegai and others in the palace was important. She didn't just focus on getting the king's attention. She obviously won the palace's favor because of her personality. They looked out for her and gave her insight and opportunities. Change requires us to have a support system that will offer us psychological safety.

- Before making a difficult decision, we must seek God in fasting and prayer. Esther asked for her community to fast but she also fasted with others close to her in the palace. We always need to seek God for discernment and guidance.
- Esther understood that she needed to assess the landscape. She knew the king's behaviors and temperament. This informed her decision-making. As we make decisions, we must conduct our own assessments.
- Having a vision is necessary. Our decisions cannot be made in isolation. I often tell my daughter that every person she sees is the sum total of their decisions. Our decisions have power. Esther had a vision beyond being queen. Her vision was to save her people.
- Esther moved from having a vision to creating a plan. She made a plan with Mordecai about how to implement the vision. Vision is important, but if we are going to be successful in any change management process, we must have a road map.
- Finally, Esther realized that obtaining buy-in was important. She had to get her community behind her. She needed their support. Building buy-in is always important. We cannot make decisions as leaders without the input of others.

Esther is a reminder that we have the ability to make an impact through our decisions. We can change things, especially when we put God first in all we do!

I was speaking with a leader who shared that she had been in her role for just a few months. In that time she'd realized that the organization, despite its strong financial standing, had some serious issues that were preventing it from serving more people in their local community. Her board didn't believe there were any problems. They saw money as the only indicator and failed to look under the hood to see how silos and lack of representation were harming the organization's potential. When I asked this leader if she had any early adopters of change in the organization, she could only name a few and wasn't sure who her advocates were on the board.

It would have been tempting for this leader to try to push through a new agenda of change on her own, but without buy-in, she would lose the few advocates she had and probably generate enemies. I encouraged her to begin by identifying the buckets her team members fell into—early adopters, those who could be swayed either way, and those who dissented (even if passively). By identifying how people view the change, you can begin to strategize to make the early adopters your cheerleaders. For those who are in the middle, by discovering what they need in order to get on board, you can begin to move them to some level of agreement. Dissenters are not just negative naysayers; they are an opportunity to lean in and learn more about what they are thinking and experiencing. Be careful of dismissing this group—there's a lot that you can learn from those who disagree. Being deliberate about input is critical for a leader's success.

SCRIPTURES TO CONSIDER

> Behold, I will do a new thing.
> It springs out now.
> Don't you know it?
> I will even make a way in the wilderness,
> and rivers in the desert. (Isaiah 43:19)

> Haven't I commanded you? Be strong and courageous. Don't be afraid. Don't be dismayed, for Yahweh your God is with you wherever you go. (Joshua 1:9)

> God is not a man, that he should lie,
> nor a son of man, that he should repent.
> Has he said, and he won't do it?
> Or has he spoken, and he won't make it good?
> (Numbers 23:19)

QUESTIONS FOR REFLECTION

1. How do you identify with Esther's journey?
2. What are your barriers to creating the change you want to see in your life?
3. When have you had to coach up? What happened?

PRAYER

God, you never promised us an easy life, but you did say you would always be with us. Change can be scary. We fear the unknown and desire control. You want to change us to be in the image of Christ, which means we must give up our way for yours. Help us to be comfortable with the uncomfortable and be willing to go wherever you lead us. With you, all things are possible and we can face whatever comes our way. In Jesus' name we pray, amen.

PROFILES IN LEADERSHIP

Read the Power in the Room: Mariah's Story

Mariah is a Black woman in her thirties. With two master's degrees, she worked in a number of positions before starting her own business in a male-dominated field.

"Before I started my company, I had several situations where people really underestimated me or undervalued what I brought to the table," she says. "One boss told me during my performance review—after we'd had an outstanding year of bringing in dollars, new initiatives, and new partnerships—that my biggest contribution was making sure the office had [an ethnic holiday] day off."

At that time she knew it was time to go. She was frustrated, but she also knew her value, even if others didn't. "I didn't need to be there anymore. I was working too hard not to be acknowledged, and so it was time," she says.

Mariah started her company at thirty in a space composed of older White men, many of whom are her parents' age. "Coming into this space as a young Black woman, it's like everything can be against you— age, race, gender are all stacked," she says. "Thankfully I have a business partner who is well-respected, well-capitalized, and has a very good track record. People see me and assume I'm not running the show, and it's not my deal, that they can walk all over me. But they soon learn."

Walking with God throughout this journey has been central to Mariah's success. "I have no tolerance for [disrespect]," she says. "I have had several people say, 'There are some things you can't change. You can't change being Black. You can't change being a woman. You can't change the fact that you're going into these spaces being an anomaly. So don't let this stuff bother you.'

"For me to take that advice, [knowing] this was not going to change, meant having a better walk with God," Mariah says. "It meant I had to say, 'I know who I am in the presence of the Lord.' The Lord created me. He put me in this position. God is going to work this out for me despite me. And so because he's working it out for me, I know I am supposed to be here. That means I need to believe in speaking my mind. All these things I know God has proven to me, being his child, being somebody who is surrounded by him. That is where faith has been crucial in my mental fortitude, in helping me get through the day-to-day, in dealing with doubters, even sometimes in doubting myself whether I even belong here."

Lessons for Younger Women

- "Be a listener. Observe the people around you before you say anything, because it's a lot easier to ruin your reputation by sharing concerns than it is to listen and observe. I'm not saying be silent, but understand the dynamics. See who talks most in the room. What do you know about them? Are they the highest performers? Who is actually making decisions? Is it the CEO? The CFO? Is someone an idea person or an implementer? Why does XYZ

person carry weight? What relationships do you need to cultivate to understand the dynamics?"
- "Take some time to assess and evaluate the spaces you're in and start to strategize about what it looks like to move in those spaces in a way you feel comfortable."
- "Build relationships strategically within the power dynamics, then build relationships with the people who will give you sanity. Sometimes that's the janitor or the hostess in the front office—people you can be real with after somebody says something crazy in a meeting."
- "You also need people outside of work—family and friends. You are more than your work. There are other social and community endeavors you should be a part of, so take time to cultivate those spaces and remember that the workplace is not who you are in totality."

Dealing with Racism, Sexism, and Other "Isms"

- "I've had to be firm about who I am, what value I bring to the table. It requires a strong mindset in a space where I don't always want to be strong, but I know I have to be."
- "I've learned not to play small. When I started, women of color I admired would say, 'Oh, I don't like the spotlight. I just want to get the work done.' That was my thought too—why share all this stuff? Then I started to realize that people cannot give you credit where credit is due if they don't know what you're doing. It may feel cringy, but sometimes we have to be our own advocates and share the things we are doing. Often the people spotlighting themselves are no smarter than us. So I've learned to share my wins."
- "When I left my last job and sent my last email, I spent a lot of time quantifying my impact—everyone got that in my going-away email, and there were receipts. I think more women of color should consider that. There's work you're doing you can be proud of."

- "A couple of times I've been absolutely dismissed in a meeting. I've had to be very direct with some people. I've had some come-to-Jesus meetings that required me to stand up for myself. It's important to know how to speak with people in love but to set expectations for how you should be treated. That wouldn't happen if I was a man. It would not happen if I wasn't young. It would not happen with other people. It's hard for me to command a room of mainly White men who are basically my dad's age without somebody else coming in and saying, 'No, this is who's leading the group.' Having a great business partner and advocates in this space is critical."

Epilogue

Time to Go Inside from the Porch

WHEN I WAS A CHILD, we would visit my mother's godmother, Momma Gussie, in an area of Shreveport called Stoner Hill. I always thought it was "Stony Hill" because of the Southern drawl—I didn't realize this community's real name until I was an adult! But that community holds many memories for me. My mother grew up there, and I remember visiting my grandmother there before my parents moved her to another community. My aunt's family lived there as well. We would visit her mother, who we called Sister, and her grandmother, Ms. Doll, who was like a living doll to me. I grew up in the presence of many strong Black women who were oppressed by their environments.

In the Stoner Hill community the streets were lined with front porches that were screened in and often had swings. It was the place where the women sat and talked. Little girls would get their hair combed on the porch, and I could listen to the grown folks talk about their journeys. I sat on their front porches watching, listening, and waiting for more nuggets of knowledge. I learned much from these women. The porch was a safe place to hang out, laugh, and learn. Yet, when it was time, they all left to go back to their lives.

I hope that after reading this book, you are empowered to return to your life with the tools, knowledge, and support you need to endure the environments you face. Things have come a long way for women of color, and yet there is still much to be done. Come to the porch when you need a break and a breather, but at some point we must go back into homes, jobs, and communities that can be cold and difficult.

You are not alone. You are a light. Shine your light and bring others in so we can change these spaces that are not showing God's love and glory. We have an opportunity to do something different from the women of Stoner Hill and other communities. Whatever happens in politics or the media or our society, we will be fine. This isn't a time to get comfortable. We leave the porch to worship, to work, to be well, and to fight as necessary.

Know that with God, everything is possible.

As believers, our lives are in God's hands.

Acknowledgments

WRITING IS SHARING A DEEP PART OF YOUR SOUL; it is exposing your thoughts and allowing yourself to be vulnerable. As much as we may want to share our stories and insights, there is always some apprehension of the way others will interpret and receive it. I am blessed because regardless of the possibilities and outcomes, I have supporters who have loved me through many seasons.

First and foremost, I want to thank God. I am very aware and adamant that anything I have, anything I am given to do, is all a gift from my Father, God. I do not take my blessings lightly and I pray that this book glorifies God and displays God's glory and goodness in my life.

Next, I am thankful for my mother, Dorothy Booker. It has been wonderful to have her living with me for the past few years. My mother is my rock, my cheerleader, and the person who reminds me of who I am and whose I am on the days I am anxious and question myself. I love my mother profoundly; she is my best friend, confidante, and road dog.

My daughter, Kazai, is much more than my child—she has become an adviser and an employee too. She possesses much wisdom at a young age. I trust her guidance, and she is always stretching me to be better and do better. She is brilliant, and she is the best thing I have ever done in my life. There are no accomplishments that compare to this Godsend who enriches my life.

I am thankful for and to my family, who has always been there for me. Thank you to my Aunt Theresa for making me smile because of the many ways she celebrates me. Thank you to my Uncle Mac who is a deep, insightful conversationalist and a sharp-dressed man in his eighties. Thank you to my cousin Kim, her husband, Renauld, and their kids, Kalaeb and Rileigh. Kim and her fraternal twin brother, Kevin, have been like my own babies since day one and Kim has never let me go. I love her and she will always be like my child. Thank you to my cousin Reggie, who is my boy! Reggie and I are both entrepreneurs and were heavily influenced by my father and his business savvy. I am grateful for the relationship and special bond we have. Many cousins in Houston are too numerous to name, but I am grateful for how they have loved me over the years.

Thank you to my tribe.

I am thankful for Nathaniel, his kind text messages, and his words of encouragement that exude love, kindness, and admiration. He has been a part of my journey since we were children, and we have experienced a lot together as adults. Thank you, Nathaniel, for what you bring to my life. Thank you to my three best friends, Deirdre, Shene, and Lillian Denise—they have all been in my life since middle school. They are the best friends anyone could ask for and have been major blessings in my life. Thank you to my college sister, Tavia, for her ongoing support. Thank you to my community and nonprofit sisters who are in these streets making a difference: the Ashleys, Candace, Thana, Bemnet, Shawana, Leah, Kapreta, Sherri, Kim, Porsha, Cherie, Crystee, LaToyia, Angie, Jarie, Annam, HERitage sisters, and many more, including my brother from another mother, Donald Ray!

Thank you to all the case study participants; your input was invaluable.

Thank you to the mentors and elders who have given me wisdom and protection: Vicki, Cynt, Matrice, Dr. Dulaney, Pastor Chris and my Cornerstone church family, Clyde, Willie Mae Coleman, Diane

Ragsdale, Dr. Terry Flowers, Greg Campbell, Jim Scoggin—each of you has deposited such goodness into my life.

Love to you, Tori and Paula—y'all are family.

Last but definitely not least, thank you InterVarsity Press. You were a dream that came true. Years ago I wanted to publish with you all and it didn't work out at the time, but God had a plan and in due season, Al Hsu showed up and encouraged me to write once again. Thank you, Nilwona and the entire team who made this a reality!

Appendix

Resources for Connection

HERE IS A CURATED LIST OF RESOURCES designed to support and uplift women of color in leadership roles. From networking opportunities to mentorship to leadership development, these tools provide connection, growth, and empowerment for women navigating professional and personal challenges.

ASPIRE

ASPIRE is a community and mentorship program exclusively for Asian American women. It provides a well-rounded experience, offering individualized mentoring for tailored direction, group mentoring for mutual encouragement and teamwork, and growth workshops for improving abilities and self-improvement. Find more details at www.girlsaspire.org.

BLACK CAREER WOMEN'S NETWORK

A nationwide group committed to helping Black women progress in their professions across different sectors, this initiative features a wide-ranging group of mentors from various career stages and areas who give unmatched direction and assistance. At frequently held career management workshops, women receive knowledge on how to grow their professional networks and boost their visibility. In addition, the organization provides its signature Career Smarts 365 program, which brings together workbooks, strategic advice sessions, and access to a private online community promoting personal and professional development. Find more at www.bcwnetwork.com.

DREAM MENTORSHIP

This nonprofit initiative is aimed at empowering women worldwide by providing free mentorship and professional development opportunities in North America, West Africa, and Asia. They are committed to helping women pursue their aspirations and create the life they envision. See www.dreammentorship.org.

FORTÉ FOUNDATION

Through Forté, women can discover many career paths accessible in the business world, spanning diverse industries such as health care and hospitality. They can also acquire universally applicable skills that will propel their careers forward and enable them to flourish as leaders. Visit www.fortefoundation.org to learn more.

HISPANIC 100

This platform was created to empower driven Latino individuals between eighteen and twenty-four years old to prosper as business leaders and community advocates. It accomplishes this by linking them with successful Latino professionals who are part of the Hispanic 100 group, cultivating mentoring connections that direct and motivate their journey to accomplishment. Visit www.h100foundation.org.

RAISE WOMEN

The mission of this organization is to connect 100,000 women of color in the media and technology industries with accomplished female leaders who can guide them in advancing their careers and breaking down barriers. Raise Women aims to provide women with the mentorship, resources, and support they need to succeed and climb the professional ladder effectively. Visit www.raisewomen.com.

UNLOCK HER POTENTIAL

This organization—founded by Sophia Chang, author of *The Baddest B'&%$ in the Room: A Memoir* (New York: Catapult, 2020)—was created in response to the lack of women of color in senior positions. Those aspiring to C-suite positions will benefit from the mentorship and support provided by this organization. Visit www.unlockherpotential.com.

WOMEN WHO CREATE

Founded by women of color, Women Who Create is a mentorship program designed to empower young women of color in the creative industries. A number of successful and experienced mentors in various creative fields provide guidance and support to young women through this program. Visit www.womenwhocreate.org.

Further Reading

arabekian. "Three Colors of Worldview." KnowledgeWorkx, February 20, 2020. www.knowledgeworkx.com/post/three-colors-of-worldview.

Asia Society. "Asian Americans Then and Now." Asia Society, 2019. https://asiasociety.org/education/asian-americans-then-and-now.

Belcourt, Annie and the University of Montana/The Conversation. "The Hidden Health Inequalities That Indigenous Peoples Face." *High Country News*, January 26, 2018. www.hcn.org/articles/tribal-affairs-the-hidden-health-inequalities-that-indigenous-peoples-face.

Cain, Susan. *Quiet: The Power of Introverts in a World That Can't Stop Talking*. New York: Crown, 2013.

Colton, Samantha. "Dove Partners with LinkedIn in support of The CROWN Act to Help End Race-Based Hair Discrimination in the WorkplaceUSA." Dove, February 16, 2023. www.thecrownact.com/all-press/dove-partners-with-linkedin-in-support-of-the-crown-act-to-help-end-race-based-hair-discrimination-in-the-workplaceusa.

Council on Foreign Relations. "Timeline: U.S.-Mexico Relations." Council on Foreign Relations, 2023. www.cfr.org/timeline/us-mexico-relations.

Equal Justice Initiative. "Jul. 15, 1954: U.S. Government Stages Mass Deportations in the American Southwest." On This Day. Equal Justice Initiative, accessed November 17, 2024. https://calendar.eji.org/racial-injustice/jul/15.

Gutiérrez, Gabriella, Yolanda Flores Niemann, Carmen G. González, and Angela P. Harris, eds. *Presumed Incompetent*. Denver, CO: Utah State University Press, 2012.

Hirst, K. Kris. "Mississippians Were the Mound Builders in North America." ThoughtCo., February 6, 2019. www.thoughtco.com/mississippian-culture-moundbuilder-171721.

History.com Editors. "Hispanic History Milestones: Timeline." History. A&E Television Networks, updated September 15, 2023. www.history.com/topics/hispanic-history/hispanic-latinx-milestones.

History.com Editors. "Native American History Timeline." History. A&E Television Networks, updated November 18, 2024. www.history.com/topics/native-american-history/native-american-timeline.

Huang, Jess, Alexis Krivkovich, Ishanaa Rambachan, and Lareina Yee. "For Mothers in the Workplace, a Year (and Counting) like No Other." McKinsey & Company, May 5, 2021. www.mckinsey.com/featured-insights/diversity-and-inclusion/for-mothers-in-the-workplace-a-year-and-counting-like-no-other.

Judd, Donald. "Biden Becomes First President to Issue Proclamation Marking Indigenous Peoples' Day." CNN, October 8, 2021. www.cnn.com/2021/10/08/politics/indigenous-peoples-day-joe-biden/index.html.

Lowe-MacAuley, Kimberli. "Salary Negotiation: How to Find a Job's Fair Market Value." Articles on Finding a Job. FlexJobs, October 9, 2024. www.flexjobs.com/blog/post/how-to-research-the-fair-market-value-of-a-job.

McCrary, Jamie. "From Pay Gap to Pay Equity." Kogod School of Business. American University, May 6, 2022. https://kogod.american.edu/news/from-pay-gap-to-pay-equity.

McDuffie, Candace. "New Survey Reveals 25 Percent of Black Women Were Denied Job Interviews Because of Their Hair." *The Root*, March 24, 2023. www.theroot.com/new-survey-reveals-25-percent-of-black-women-were-denie-1850261432.

McHugh, Adam S. *Introverts in the Church*. Downers Grove, IL: InterVarsity Press, 2017.

National Park Service. "The Modern Civil Rights Movement, 1954-1964." Civil Rights. National Park Service, December 6, 2022. www.nps.gov/subjects/civilrights/modern-civil-rights-movement.htm.

Parker, Kim, and Cary Funk. "Gender Discrimination Comes in Many Forms for Today's Working Women." Pew Research Center, December 14, 2017. www.pewresearch.org/short-reads/2017/12/14/gender-discrimination-comes-in-many-forms-for-todays-working-women.

Rummler, Orion. "Asian American Advocates Fear New Attacks on Women and Older Adults After COVID-19 Origin Report." *The 19th*, August 30, 2021. https://19thnews.org/2021/08/asian-americans-covid-19-origin-report/.

Salam Islam. "Hagar: A Traveller to Allah." Salam Islam, January 11, 2021. https://salamislam.com/articles/lifestyle/hagar-traveller-allah.

Staglin, Garen. "Trauma at the Workplace, What to Do About It." *Forbes*, November 10, 2021. www.forbes.com/sites/onemind/2021/11/10/trauma-at-the-workplace--and-what-to-do-about-it/.

Stewart, Emily. "Women Are Burned Out at Work and at Home." Vox, May 18, 2020. www.vox.com/policy-and-politics/2020/5/18/21260209/facebook-sheryl-sandberg-interview-lean-in-women-coronavirus.

"Text of Indian Civil Rights Act." Tribal Court Clearinghouse, accessed November 17, 2024. www.tribal-institute.org/lists/icra1968.htm.

Zeidan, Adam. "Ishmael." *Encyclopædia Britannica*, November 18, 2024. www.britannica.com/biography/Ishmael-son-of-Abraham.

Notes

FOREWORD

[1] Michelle Obama, "Michelle Obama Is Tired of 'Watching Men Fail Up,'" interview by Tracee Ellis Ross, YouTube, May 6, 2018, www.youtube.com/watch?v=P-qAJnISJYM.

1. WHAT DO LEADERSHIP, WOMEN, AND WORK HAVE TO DO WITH IT?

[1] Carolyn Custis James, "The Ezer-Kenegdo: Ezer Unleashed" (blog), FaithGateway, accessed September 2, 2024, https://faithgateway.com/blogs/christian-books/ezer-unleashed.

2. WHAT DOES THE DATA SAY?

[1] "Women of Color in the United States (Quick Take)," Catalyst, February 1, 2023, www.catalyst.org/insights/2023/women-of-color-in-the-united-states.
[2] Saul McLeod, "Maslow's Hierarchy of Needs," SimplyPsychology, January 24, 2024, www.simplypsychology.org/maslow.html.
[3] "Women of Color."
[4] "Race to Lead: An Initiative of Building Movement Project," Race to Lead, accessed August 13, 2024, https://racetolead.org.
[5] Ofronama Biu, *Race to Lead: Women of Color in the Nonprofit Sector* (n.p.: Race to Lead: Building Movement Project, 2019), https://racetolead.org/women-of-color.
[6] Amy Rigby, "Women of Color in the Workplace: Why Representation Matters," Marlee, accessed August 13, 2024, www.fingerprintforsuccess.com/blog/women-of-color-in-the-workplace.
[7] Emily Field, Alexis Krivkovich, Lareina Yee, Nicole Robinson, and Sandra Kügele, "Women in the Workplace 2023." McKinsey & Company and LeanIn.Org, October 5, 2023, www.mckinsey.com/featured-insights/diversity-and-inclusion/women-in-the-workplace-2023.

[8] Molly Bohannon, "Fortune 500 Board Seats for Women and People of Color Surge—But There's Still Progress Needed, Report Says," *Forbes*, June 15, 2023, www.forbes.com/sites/mollybohannon/2023/06/15/fortune-500-board-seats-for-women-and-people-of-color-surge-but-theres-still-progress-needed-report-says.

[9] "Sandra Douglass Morgan," Las Vegas Raiders, accessed November 17, 2024, www.raiders.com/team/front-office-roster/sandra-douglass-morgan.

[10] Froswa' Booker, "The Impact of Cynt Marshall's Leadership," *Dallas Morning News*, October 11, 2024, www.dallasnews.com/opinion/commentary/2024/10/11/the-impact-of-cynt-marshalls-leadership/.

[11] Caroline Fairchild, "Fortune 500's First Latina CEO Speaks Out on Climbing the Corporate Ladder," Lean In, June 13, 2024, https://leanin.org/article/first-latina-ceo-fortune-500.

[12] "5 Companies with Hispanic and Latino CEOs." Resources (blog), AboveBoard, September 14, 2022, https://blog.aboveboard.com/hispanic-latino-ceos.

[13] "Priscilla Almodovar," Fannie Mae, accessed November 17, 2024, www.fanniemae.com/about-us/fannie-mae-leadership-team/priscilla-almodovar.

[14] LA Stories Staff, "Dorene Dominguez on Breaking the Mold as a Latina CEO and NBA Team Owner," Spectrum News 1, October 23, 2023, https://spectrumnews1.com/ca/southern-california/la-stories/2023/10/21/la-stories--latina-ceo-and-nba-team-owner-dorene-dominguez.

[15] Steve Henson, "Kim Ng, First Female General Manager, Leaves Marlins for Same Reason Derek Jeter Did," *Los Angeles Times*, October 16, 2023, www.latimes.com/sports/story/2023-10-16/kim-ng-leaves-marlins-general-manager-dodgers-yankees-red-sox-mets.

[16] Kimmy Yam, "Natalie Nakase Becomes WNBA's First Asian American Head Coach," NBC News, October 11, 2024, www.nbcnews.com/news/asian-america/natalie-nakase-golden-state-valkyries-first-asian-american-head-coach-rcna175045.

[17] Daniel Thomas Mollenkamp, "Top Native American CEOs," Investopedia, July 25, 2024, www.investopedia.com/top-native-american-ceos-6746279.

[18] Katherine Schaeffer, "22 States Have Ever Elected a Black Woman to Congress," Pew Research Center, February 16, 2023, www.pewresearch.org/short-reads/2023/02/16/22-states-have-ever-elected-a-black-woman-to-congress.

[19] Matt Gonzales, "Women of Color in Federal Jobs: Less Pay, Fewer Promotions," SHRM, December 1, 2023, www.shrm.org/topics-tools/news/women-of-color-in-federal-jobs-less-pay-fewer-promotions.

[20] Kimberly Nelms Smarr, Rachelle Disbennett-Lee, and Amy Cooper Hakim, "Gender and Race in Ministry Leadership: Experiences of Black Clergywomen," *Religions* 9, no. 12 (2018): 377, https://doi.org/10.3390/rel9120377.

21. Erin Kane, "Women of Color Less Than 4% of UMC Clergy," ResourceUMC, accessed September 1, 2024, www.resourceumc.org/en/partners/gcsrw/home/content/women-of-color-less-than-4-of-umc-clergy.

22. Eileen Campbell-Reed, "State of Clergywomen in the U.S.: A Statistical Update, October 2018," 2018, https://cdn.eileencampbellreed.org/wp-content/uploads/Downloads/State-of-Clergywomen-US-2018-web.pdf.

23. The Associated Press, "Grant Program for Black Women Business Owners Is Discriminatory, Appeals Court Rules." *NPR*, June 3, 2024, www.npr.org/2024/06/03/g-s1-2649/fearless-fund-grant-program-appeal-ruling.

24. Char Adams and Nigel Chiwaya, "Map: See Which States Have Introduced or Passed Anti-DEI Bills," NBC News, March 2, 2024, www.nbcnews.com/data-graphics/anti-dei-bills-states-republican-lawmakers-map-rcna140756.

25. Sara Lindsay, Sharon Epperson, and Lindsey Jacobson, "How Companies Are Fulfilling Promises Made Following George Floyd's Murder," CNBC, January 21, 2023, www.cnbc.com/2023/01/21/how-companies-are-fulfilling-promises-made-after-george-floyds-murder.html.

26. Taylor Telford, "As DEI Gets More Divisive, Companies Are Ditching Their Teams," *Washington Post*, February 18, 2024, www.washingtonpost.com/business/2024/02/20/corporate-diversity-job-cuts.

3. YOU ARE NOT AN IMPOSTOR

1. Pauline Rose Clance and Suzanne Ament Imes, "The Impostor Phenomenon in High Achieving Women: Dynamics and Therapeutic Intervention," *Psychotherapy: Theory, Research and Practice* 15, no. 3 (Fall 1978): 241-47, https://mpowir.org/wp-content/uploads/2010/02/Download-IP-in-High-Achieving-Women.pdf.

2. K. Cokley et al., "Impostor Feelings as a Moderator and Mediator of the Relationship Between Perceived Discrimination and Mental Health Among Racial/Ethnic Minority College Students," *Journal of Counseling Psychology*, 64, no. 2 (2017): 141-54, https://doi.org/10.1037/cou0000198.

3. Martin R. Huecker et al., "Imposter Phenomenon," in *StatPearls* (Treasure Island, FL: StatPearls Publishing, 2023), https://pubmed.ncbi.nlm.nih.gov/36251839.

4. A. Rochaun Meadows-Fernandez, "Why Won't Society Let Black Girls Be Children?," *New York Times*, April 17, 2020, www.nytimes.com/2020/04/17/parenting/adultification-black-girls.html.

5. Marianne Williamson, *A Return to Love: Reflections on the Principles of a Course in Miracles* (New York: HarperCollins, 2014), 144.

6. Cheryl L. Woods-Giscombé, "Superwoman Schema: African American Women's Views on Stress, Strength, and Health," *Qualitative Health Research* 20, no. 5 (2010): 668-83, https://doi.org/10.1177/1049732310361892.

[7] Ninochka McTaggart et al., "Representations of Black Women in Hollywood," Geena Davis Institute for Gender in Media, 2021, https://geenadavisinstitute.org/research/representations-of-black-women-in-hollywood.

[8] Andrea Puente, "Media's Portrayal of Latinas," *Controversial Media* (blog), June 23, 2009, http://controversialmedia.blogspot.com/2009/06/medias-portrayal-of-latinas.html.

[9] Michael Haynes, "Latino Stereotypes in Television," *2018 Symposium*, 31, https://dc.ewu.edu/scrw_2018/31.

[10] S. Mukkamala and K. L. Suyemoto, "Racialized Sexism/Sexualized Racism: A Multimethod Study of Intersectional Experiences of Discrimination for Asian American Women," *Asian American Journal of Psychology* 9, no. 1 (March): 32-46, https://doi.org/10.1037/aap0000104.

[11] Rebecca Nagle, "Media Representation of Native Women: Invisibility, Stereotypes, Whitewashing," Women's Media Center, June 12, 2018, https://womensmediacenter.com/news-features/media-representation-of-native-women-invisibility-stereotypes-whitewashing.

[12] Ruchika Tulshyan and Jodi-Ann Burey, "Stop Telling Women They Have Imposter Syndrome," *Harvard Business Review*, February 11, 2021, https://hbr.org/2021/02/stop-telling-women-they-have-imposter-syndrome.

4. WHO YOU NEED IN LIFE

[1] Katy Dickinson, Tanya Jankot, and Helen Gracon, *Sun Mentoring: 1996–2009* (Menlo Park, CA: Sun Microsystems, 2009), www.mentoringstandard.com/wp-content/uploads/2020/06/2009-Sun-Mentoring-1996-2000-Dickinson.pdf.

[2] "Mentoring Women of Color, Particularly in STEM," *Mentoring & Tutoring: Partnership in Learning* 24, no. 5 (2016): 341-45, https://doi.org/10.1080/13611267.2016.1285388.

[3] Juanita Johnson-Bailey, Tennille Lasker-Scott, and Yolanda Sealey-Ruiz, "Mentoring While Black & Female: The Gendered Literacy Phenomenon of Black Women Mentors" (paper presented at Adult Education Research Conference, Manhattan, KS, 2015), https://newprairiepress.org/aerc/2015/papers/29.

[4] Rosalind Chow, "Don't Just Mentor Women and People of Color. Sponsor Them," *Harvard Business Review*, June 30, 2021, https://hbr.org/2021/06/dont-just-mentor-women-and-people-of-color-sponsor-them.

[5] Melissa Eisler, "Your Personal Board of Directors," Wide Lens Leadership, June 16, 2022, https://widelensleadership.com/your-personal-board-of-directors.

5. REJECTION AND TRAUMA IN THE WORKPLACE

[1] Kim Elsesser, "Women's Reaction to Rejection May Be Keeping Them out of the Corner Office," *Forbes*, February 7, 2017, www.forbes.com/sites/kimelsesser/2017/02/07/womens-reaction-to-rejection-may-be-keeping-them-out-of-the-corner-office.

[2] Ron Todt, "Acting Temple University President JoAnne A. Epps Dies after Falling Ill on Stage," AP News, September 19, 2023, https://apnews.com/article/temple-university-president-dies-77bd937e8f958d0f7134ab7a6f78b753.

[3] Alexia Hudson-Ward, "Two Black Women University Presidents Have Died, Spurring Heartrending Accounts of Workplace Discrimination," Choice 360, September 27, 2023, www.choice360.org/tie-post/two-black-women-university-presidents-have-died-spurring-heartrending-accounts-of-workplace-discrimination.

[4] Yolanda Flores Niemann, Gabriella Gutiérrez y Muhs, and Carmen G. González, eds., *Presumed Incompetent II: Race, Class, Power, and Resistance of Women in Academia* (Louisville, CO: Utah State University Press, 2020).

[5] Ronald C. Kessler et al., "Trauma and PTSD in the WHO World Mental Health Surveys," *European Journal of Psychotraumatology* 8 (sup5), https://doi.org/10.1080/20008198.2017.1353383.

[6] "Trauma," American Psychological Association, accessed September 2, 2024, www.apa.org/topics/trauma.

[7] Reagan Myers and Brienne Adams, "The Color Purple by Alice Walker: Summary, Analysis & Quotes," Study.com, November 21, 2023, https://study.com/learn/lesson/the-color-purple.html.

[8] Joy DeGruy, "Post Traumatic Slave Syndrome," Dr. Joy DeGruy, accessed September 2, 2024, www.joydegruy.com/post-traumatic-slave-syndrome.

[9] Chu Kim-Prieto et al., "Legacies of War: Asian American Women and War Trauma," *Women & Therapy* 41, no. 3-4 (2018): 203-18, https://doi.org/10.1080/02703149.2018.1425023.

[10] Ramsay Liem, "Silencing Historical Trauma: The Politics and Psychology of Memory and Voice," *Peace and Conflict: Journal of Peace Psychology* 13, no. 2 (2007): 153-74, https://doi.org/10.1080/10781910701271200.

[11] Jieyi Cai and Richard M. Lee, "Intergenerational Communication About Historical Trauma in Asian American Families," *Adversity and Resilience Science* 3 (2022): 233-45, https://doi.org/10.1007/s42844-022-00064-y.

[12] Yael Danieli, Fran H. Norris, and Brian Engdahl, "Multigenerational Legacies of Trauma: Modeling the What and How of Transmission," *American Journal of Orthopsychiatry* 86, no. 6 (2016): 639-51, https://doi.org/10.1037/ort0000145.

[13] N. J. Lin and K. L. Suyemoto, "*So You, My Children, Can Have a Better Life*: A Cambodian American Perspective on the Phenomenology of Intergenerational Communication About Trauma," *Journal of Aggression, Maltreatment*

and Trauma 25, no. 4 (2016): 400-420, https://doi.org/10.1080/10926771.2015.1133748.

[14]"Immigrant Rights and Reproductive Justice: How Harsh Immigration Policies Harm Immigrant Health," National Women's Law Center, April 2017, https://nwlc.org/wp-content/uploads/2017/04/Immigrant-Rights-and-Reproductive-Justice.pdf.

[15]Lisa R. Fortuna et al., "Trauma, Immigration, and Sexual Health Among Latina Women: Implications for Maternal-Child Well-Being and Reproductive Justice," *Infant Mental Health Journal* 40, no. 5 (2019): 640-58, https://doi.org/10.1002/imhj.21805.

[16]Michael S. Scheeringa et al., "Trauma-Focused Cognitive-Behavioral Therapy for Posttraumatic Stress Disorder in Three-Through Six Year-Old Children: A Randomized Clinical Trial," *Journal of Child Psychology and Psychiatry* 52, no. 8 (August 2011): 853-60, https://doi.org/10.1111/j.1469-7610.2010.02354.x.

[17]Rachel Yehuda et al., "Holocaust Exposure Induced Intergenerational Effects on FKBP5 Methylation," *Biological Psychiatry* 80, no. 5 (September 1, 2016): 372-80, https://doi.org/10.1016/j.biopsych.2015.08.005.

[18]Gloria D. Thomas and Carol Hollenshead, "Resisting from the Margins: The Coping Strategies of Black Women and Other Women of Color Faculty Members at a Research University," *The Journal of Negro Education* 70, no. 3 (2001): 166-75, https://doi.org/10.2307/3211208.

[19]Kenneth R. Williams, "The Cost of Tolerating Toxic Behaviors in the Department of Defense Workplace," *Military Review*, July-August 2019, www.armyupress.army.mil/Journals/Military-Review/English-Edition-Archives/July-August-2019/Williams-Toxic-Behavior.

[20]Mitchell Kusy and Elizabeth Holloway, *Toxic Workplace!: Managing Toxic Personalities and Their Systems of Power* (San Francisco: Jossey-Bass, 2009).

[21]Lee G. Bolman and Terrence E. Deal, *Reframing Organizations: Artistry, Choice, and Leadership* (San Francisco: Jossey-Bass, 2013).

[22]Adapted from Christin, "A Prayer for Those Who Have Been Rejected," Garments of Splendor, January 11, 2019, https://garmentsofsplendor.com/a-prayer-for-those-who-have-been-rejected.

6. INTERSECTIONALITY AND LEADERSHIP

[1]Katy Steinmetz, "She Coined the Term 'Intersectionality' Over 30 Years Ago. Here's What It Means to Her Today," *Time*, February 20, 2020, https://time.com/5786710/kimberle-crenshaw-intersectionality.

[2]Nyasha Junior, *Reimagining Hagar: Blackness and Bible* (Oxford: Oxford University Press, 2019).

[3]Tivka Frymer-Kensky, updated by Tamar Kamionkowski, "Hagar: Bible," *The Shalvi/Hyman Encyclopedia of Jewish Women*, Jewish Women's Archive, June 23, 2021, https://jwa.org/encyclopedia/article/hagar-bible.

⁴"About: Hagar in Islam," DBpedia, accessed September 2, 2024, https://dbpedia.org/page/Hagar_in_Islam.
⁵Dan P. McAdams, "Narrative Identity," in Seth J. Schwartz, Koen Luyckx, and Vivian L. Vignoles, *Handbook of Identity Theory and Research* (New York: Springer, 2011), 1, 99-115, https://doi.org/10.1007/978-1-4419-7988-9_5.
⁶"Exploring the Concept of Identity," Facing History and Ourselves, July 14, 2021, www.facinghistory.org/resource-library/exploring-concept-identity.

7. NETWORKING AND SOCIAL CAPITAL

¹Gwen Moore, "Structural Determinants of Men's and Women's Personal Networks," *American Sociological Review* 55, no. 5 (October 1990): 726, https://doi.org/10.2307/2095868.
²Pierre Bourdieu, "The Forms of Capital," in *Readings in Economic Sociology*, Nicole Woolsey Biggart, ed., (Hoboken, NJ: Wiley-Blackwell, 2002), 4, 281, https://doi.org/10.1002/9780470755679.ch15.
³Robert D. Putnam, Robert Leonardi, and Raffaella Y. Nanetti, *Making Democracy Work: Civic Traditions in Modern Italy* (Princeton, NJ: Princeton University Press, 1993), 167.
⁴Jenepher Lennox Terrion, "The Development of Social Capital Through a Leadership Training Program," Mountainrise 3, no. 2 (January 2006): 1-14. www.researchgate.net/publication/251375314.
⁵Ronald S. Burt, "The Gender of Social Capital," *Rationality and Society* 10, no. 1 (1998): 5-46, https://doi.org/10.1177/104346398010001001.
⁶Tsedale M. Melaku, Angie Beeman, David G. Smith, and W. Brad Johnson, "Be a Better Ally," *Harvard Business Review* (November–December 2020), https://hbr.org/2020/11/be-a-better-ally.

8. EMOTIONAL AND SPIRITUAL INTELLIGENCE AS A STRATEGY

¹"What Is Emotional Intelligence and How Does It Apply to the Workplace?," Mental Health America, accessed September 2, 2024, https://mhanational.org/what-emotional-intelligence-and-how-does-it-apply-workplace.
²"EI Overview: The Four Domains and Twelve Competencies," Daniel Goleman Emotional Intelligence Courses, accessed November 15, 2024, https://danielgolemanemotionalintelligence.com/ei-overview-the-four-domains-and-twelve-competencies.
³Taryn Fuchs, "Expanding Your Emotional Vocabulary," The Conflict Center, April 10, 2019, https://conflictcenter.org/expanding-your-emotional-vocabulary.
⁴Peter Salovey and John D. Mayer, "Emotional Intelligence," *Imagination, Cognition and Personality* 9, no. 3 (March 1990): 185-211, https://doi.org/10.2190/DUGG-P24E-52WK-6CDG.

5. Thomas Maak and Nicola M. Pless, "Business Leaders as Citizens of the World. Advancing Humanism on a Global Scale," *Journal of Business Ethics* 88, no. 3 (2009): 537-50, https://doi.org/10.1007/s10551-009-0122-0.

6. Robert Kegan, *The Evolving Self: Problem and Process in Human Development* (Cambridge: Harvard University Press, 1982), 18.

7. Kegan, *Evolving Self*, 34.

8. Arlie Russell Hochschild, *The Managed Heart: Commercialization of Human Feeling* (Berkeley: University of California Press, 1983).

9. Fred Luthans, Bruce J. Avolio, James B. Avey, and Steven M. Norman, "Positive Psychological Capital: Measurement and Relationship with Performance and Satisfaction," *Personnel Psychology* 60, no. 3 (2007): 541-72, https://doi.org/10.1111/j.1744-6570.2007.00083.x.

10. Kate Bowles, "Narrative Therapy and Critical Reflection on Practice: A Conversation with Jan Fook," *Journal of Systemic Therapies*, 2011, www.academia.edu/88619851.

11. Amanda Sinclair, *Leadership for the Disillusioned: Moving Beyond Myths and Heroes to Leading That Liberates* (Crows Nest, NSW: Allen & Unwin, 2007).

12. Richard J. Martinez, Robin Rogers, Gaynor Yancey, and Jon Singletary, "Spiritual Capital in Modern Organizations," *Journal of Biblical Integration in Business* 13, no. 1 (2011), https://doi.org/10.69492/jbib.v13i1.199.

13. Sheila Barssel, Emily Shaffer, and Dnika J. Travis, *Emotional Tax and Work Teams: A View from 5 Countries*, Catalyst, 2022, www.catalyst.org/reports/emotional-tax-teams.

14. Hochschild, *Managed Heart*, 1983.

15. Tait Manning, "Emotional Labor of Women of Color in the Workplace," WorkEnlightened, August 10, 2021, https://medium.com/workenlightened/emotional-labor-of-women-of-color-in-the-workplace-5902836cfa34.

16. Carolyn M. West, "Mammy, Sapphire, and Jezebel: Historical Images of Black Women and Their Implications for Psychotherapy," *Psychotherapy* 32, no. 3 (1995): 458-66, https://works.bepress.com/carolyn_west/43.

17. Stephany Payne, "The Effects of Emotional Dissonance on African American Female Officers When Their Cultural Identity Is Threatened," abstract (PhD diss., University of LaVerne, 2013), https://researchworks.laverne.edu/esploro/outputs/doctoral/The-effects-of-emotional-dissonance-on/991004156151206311.

18. Rania Siddique, "'At What Cost?': Women of Color Therapists and Emotional Labor," (bachelor's thesis, Barnard College, 2018), https://doi.org/10.7916/d8tm8tjt.

9. DISCRIMINATION IN THE WORKPLACE

[1] "Is Texas an At-Will Employment State?," Ross, Scalise, Beeler and Pillischer Employment Lawyers, accessed September 2, 2024, www.rosslawgroup.com/is-texas-an-at-will-employment-state.

[2] "The Pregnant Workers Fairness Act: Fact Sheet," National Partnership for Women & Families, February 2021, www.nationalpartnership.org/our-work/resources/economic-justice/pregnancy-discrimination/fact-sheet-pwfa.pdf.

[3] "Pregnant Workers Fairness Act."

[4] Ceri Parker, "It's Official: Women Work Nearly an Hour Longer Than Men Every Day," World Economic Forum, June 1, 2017, www.weforum.org/agenda/2017/06/its-official-women-work-nearly-an-hour-longer-than-men-every-day.

[5] U.S. Bureau of Labor Statistics, "Women in the Labor Force: A Databook, Report 1092," BLS Reports: U.S. Bureau of Labor Statistics, April 2021, www.bls.gov/opub/reports/womens-databook/2020/home.htm.

[6] Rachel Thomas et al., "Women in the Workplace," McKinsey & Company and LeanIn.org, 2021, https://wiw-report.s3.amazonaws.com/Women_in_the_Workplace_2021.pdf.

[7] Jasmine Babers, "For Women of Color, the Glass Ceiling Is Actually Made of Concrete," Aspen Institute, April 19, 2016, www.aspeninstitute.org/blog-posts/for-women-of-color-the-glass-ceiling-is-actually-made-of-concrete.

[8] Jaclyn S. Wong and Andrew M. Penner, "Gender and the Returns to Attractiveness," *Research in Social Stratification and Mobility* 44 (April 2016): 113-23, https://doi.org/10.1016/j.rssm.2016.04.002.

[9] Jennifer Haskin, "Third Shift Appearance Work: Experiences of Career-Oriented Mothers," abstract (PhD diss., Wayne State University, 2015), https://digitalcommons.wayne.edu/oa_dissertations/1355/.

[10] "Hair Discrimination Research: Dove CROWN Studies," Dove US, December 6, 2023, www.dove.com/us/en/stories/about-dove/hair-discrimination-research.html.

[11] "Uncovering the Dangers of Hair Products Marketed to Black Women, Girls," Harvard T.H. Chan School of Public Health, June 15, 2024, https://hsph.harvard.edu/news/uncovering-the-dangers-of-hair-products-marketed-to-black-women-girls/.

[12] Ana Sandoiu, "'Weathering': What Are the Health Effects of Stress and Discrimination?," February 26, 2021, MedicalNewsToday, www.medicalnewstoday.com/articles/weathering-what-are-the-health-effects-of-stress-and-discrimination#How-the-weathering-concept-came-about.

[13] Arline T. Geronimus, *Weathering: The Extraordinary Stress of Ordinary Life in an Unjust Society* (New York: Little, Brown Spark, 2023).

10. THE POSTRACIAL SOCIETY IS AN IDEAL

[1] Nikole Hannah Jones, ed., "The 1619 Project," *New York Times Magazine*, August 14, 2019, www.nytimes.com/interactive/2019/08/14/magazine/1619-america-slavery.html.

[2] "Number of People Shot to Death by Police in the United States from 2017 to 2024, by Race," October 22, 2024, Statista, www.statista.com/statistics/585152/people-shot-to-death-by-us-police-by-race.

[3] Neil G. Ruiz, Khadijah Edwards, and Mark Hugo Lopez, "One-Third of Asian Americans Fear Threats, Physical Attacks and Most Say Violence Against Them Is Rising," *Pew Research Center*, April 14, 2021, www.pewresearch.org/short-reads/2021/04/21/one-third-of-asian-americans-fear-threats-physical-attacks-and-most-say-violence-against-them-is-rising.

[4] Nambi Ndugga, Latoya Hill, and Samantha Artiga, "Key Data on Health and Health Care by Race and Ethnicity," KFF, June 11, 2024, www.kff.org/key-data-on-health-and-health-care-by-race-and-ethnicity.

[5] Alexis Butler, Katherine Carter, and Lauren Lowery, "Embedding Racial Equity in Housing," National League of Cities, July 9, 2020, www.nlc.org/article/2020/07/09/embedding-racial-equity-in-housing.

[6] rachel, "EEOC 2023 Statistics," Employment Law Help, May 16, 2024, www.employmentlawhelp.org/blog/eeoc-2023-statistics.

[7] Stephanie Taylor, "Black Women in the Workplace: Is Human Resources a Friend or Foe?," MSN.com, May 13, 2024, www.msn.com/en-us/lifestyle/career/black-women-in-the-workplace-is-human-resources-a-friend-or-foe/ar-BB1mjSif.

[8] Mandile Mpofu, "Researchers: Higher Turnover, Lower Promotion Rates for Black Women with Predominantly White Co-Workers," *Bay State Banner*, November 13, 2024, https://baystatebanner.com/2024/11/13/researchers-higher-turnover-lower-promotion-rates-for-black-women-with-predominantly-white-co-workers/.

[9] "Women in the Workplace: Asian Women," September 2021, Lean In, https://leanin.org/article/women-in-the-workplace-asian-women.

[10] "Latinas Aren't Paid Fairly—And That's Just the Tip of the Iceberg," Lean In, accessed September 5, 2024, https://leanin.org/data-about-the-gender-pay-gap-for-latinas.

[11] Kimberly Wilson, "Black Women Lose Nearly a Million Dollars over a Lifetime Due to Gender Wage Gap," *Essence*, August 1, 2021. www.essence.com/news/money-career/black-women-lose-nearly-million-dollars-over-a-lifetime-gender-wage-gap.

[12] Dan Gunderson, "Study Finds Large Pay Gap for Native American Women," *MPR News*, November 27, 2023, www.mprnews.org/story/2023/11/27/study-finds-large-pay-gap-for-native-american-women.

¹³Santhosh, "Addressing Racism in the Workplace: Strategies for a Diverse and Inclusive Culture," CultureMonkey, May 2, 2024, www.culturemonkey.io/employee-engagement/racism-in-the-workplace.

¹⁴Rachel B. Levitt and Jessica L. Barnack-Tavlaris, "Addressing Menstruation in the Workplace: The Menstrual Leave Debate," in C. Bobel et al., eds., *The Palgrave Handbook of Critical Menstruation Studies* (Singapore: Palgrave Macmillan, 2020), 561-75, https://doi.org/10.1007/978-981-15-0614-7_43.

¹⁵Kimberly Palmer, "10 Things You Should Know About Age Discrimination," AARP, October 31, 2024, www.aarp.org/work/age-discrimination/facts-in-the-workplace.

¹⁶Stephanie S. Faubion, Felicity Enders, Mary S. Hedges, Rajeev Chaudhry, Juliana M. Kling, Chrisandra L. Shufelt, Mariam Saadedine, Kristin Mara, Joan M. Griffin, and Ekta Kapoor, "Impact of Menopause Symptoms on Women in the Workplace," *Mayo Clinic Proceedings* 98, no. 6 (June 2024): 833-45, https://doi.org/10.1016/j.mayocp.2023.02.025.

¹⁷Kelsey Butler, "How Does Menopause Affect Women in the Workplace?," *Time*, April 26, 2023, https://time.com/6274622/menopause-us-economy-women-work.

¹⁸Leslie Goldman, "For Women of Color, Menopause Is Different," Oprah Daily, April 18, 2022, www.oprahdaily.com/life/health/a39649768/women-of-color-menopause.

¹⁹Eduardo Bonilla-Silva, "Rethinking Racism: Toward a Structural Interpretation," *American Sociological Review* 62, no. 3 (June 1997): 465-80, www.jstor.org/stable/2657316.

11. INTERVIEWING, NEGOTIATING, AND GETTING THE ROLE

¹Nicquel Terry Ellis, "'Very Rarely Is It as Good as It Seems': Black Women in Leadership Are Finding Themselves on the 'Glass Cliff,'" CNN, December 17, 2022, www.cnn.com/2022/12/17/us/black-women-glass-cliff-reaj/index.html.

²Deepa Purushothaman, Deborah M. Kolb, Hannah Riley Bowles, and Valerie Purdie-Greenaway, "Negotiating as a Woman of Color," *Harvard Business Review*, January 14, 2022, https://hbr.org/2022/01/negotiating-as-a-woman-of-color.

³Suzette Haden Elgin, *What Is Linguistics?* 2nd ed. (Englewood Cliffs, NJ: Prentice Hall, 1979).

⁴Amina Dunn, "Younger, College-Educated Black Americans Are Most Likely to Feel Need to 'Code-Switch,'" Pew Research Center, September 24, 2019, www.pewresearch.org/short-reads/2019/09/24/younger-college-educated-black-americans-are-most-likely-to-feel-need-to-code-switch.

⁵Naomi Cahn, "Do Women and Men Have a Confidence Gap?," *Forbes*, February 26, 2020, www.forbes.com/sites/naomicahn/2020/02/26/do-women-and-men-have-a-confidence-gap.

⁶Ruchika Tulshyan and Jodi-Ann Burey, "Stop Telling Women They Have Imposter Syndrome," *Harvard Business Review*, February 11, 2021, https://hbr.org/2021/02/stop-telling-women-they-have-imposter-syndrome.

⁷Ellis, "'Very Rarely Is It as Good as It Seems.'"

⁸Adda Birnir, "How to Ask If a Company Supports Women of Color," Skillcrush, September 14, 2020, https://skillcrush.com/blog/how-to-ask-if-a-company-supports-women-of-color.

⁹Madeline Miles, "Understanding Pay Transparency: 5 Reasons to Start Talking Money," BetterUp, June 28, 2023, www.betterup.com/blog/pay-transparency.

¹⁰Kim Elsesser, "Women of Color Set Lower Salary Requirements than White Men, According to Job Search Site," *Forbes*, February 7, 2023, www.forbes.com/sites/kimelsesser/2023/02/06/women-of-color-set-lower-salary-requirements-than-white-men-according-to-job-search-site.

¹¹Samara Linton, "Salary Transparency Alone Isn't Enough, Black Women Need These Changes Too," POCIT: People of Color in Tech, June 27, 2023, https://peopleofcolorintech.com/articles/salary-transparency-alone-isnt-enough-black-women-need-these-changes-too.

¹²Purushothaman et al., "Negotiating as a Woman of Color."

12. THE IMPACT OF WHITE SUPREMACY ON ORGANIZATIONAL CULTURE

¹Elias Leight, "Paul McCartney Remembers 'Truly Magnificent' Fats Domino," *Rolling Stone*, October 26, 2017, www.rollingstone.com/music/music-news/paul-mccartney-remembers-truly-magnificent-fats-domino-128449.

²Amy Guthrie, "Mexico Fights Cultural Appropriation with New Intellectual Property Law," Law.com International, December 6, 2021, www.law.com/international-edition/2021/12/06/mexico-fights-cultural-appropriation-with-new-intellectual-property-law.

³Froswa' Booker-Drew, "From Bonding to Bridging: Using the Immunity to Change (ITC) Process to Build Social Capital and Create Change," (PhD diss., Antioch University, 2014), http://rave.ohiolink.edu/etdc/view?acc_num=antioch1410806690.

⁴Margaret Hunter, "The Persistent Problem of Colorism: Skin Tone, Status, and Inequality," *Sociology Compass* 100006, no. 10 (September 2007): 237-54, www.researchgate.net/publication/229056955_The_Persistent_Problem_of_Colorism_Skin_Tone_Status_and_Inequality.

⁵"For Latina Women, Health Disparities Persist," Globo, accessed September 5, 2024, www.helloglobo.com/blog/for-latina-women-health-disparities-persist.

⁶Donna Hoyert, "Maternal Mortality Rates in the United States, 2021," National Center for Health Statistics, Centers for Disease Control and Prevention,

March 16, 2023, www.cdc.gov/nchs/data/hestat/maternal-mortality/2021/maternal-mortality-rates-2021.htm.

[7] Serena Williams, "Serena Williams: What My Life-Threatening Experience Taught Me About Giving Birth," CNN, February 20, 2018, www.cnn.com/2018/02/20/opinions/protect-mother-pregnancy-williams-opinion/index.html.

[8] "2023 Demographic Differences in Federal Sentencing," United States Sentencing Commission, November 14, 2023, www.ussc.gov/research/research-reports/2023-demographic-differences-federal-sentencing.

[9] "2023 Demographic Differences."

[10] Tema Okun, "White Supremacy Culture Characteristics," White Supremacy Culture, 2021, www.whitesupremacyculture.info/characteristics.html.

[11] Peter Baker, "Bush Made Willie Horton an Issue in 1988, and the Racial Scars Are Still Fresh," New York Times, December 3, 2018, www.nytimes.com/2018/12/03/us/politics/bush-willie-horton.html.

[12] Herbert Hoover, "Principles and Ideals of the United States Government," (speech, October 22, 1928), https://teachingamericanhistory.org/document/rugged-individualism.

[13] "Lesley Lokko Explains Her Resignation from City College of New York's Spitzer School of Architecture," Architectural Record, October 5, 2020, www.architecturalrecord.com/articles/14831-lesley-lokko-explains-her-resignation-from-city-college-of-new-yorks-spitzer-school-of-architecture.

[14] Bianca Quilantan, "Harvard Governing Board, Activists Say Claudine Gay Was a Victim of Racism," Politico, January 2, 2024, www.politico.com/news/2024/01/02/harvard-presidents-resignation-fuels-accusations-of-racism-from-black-leaders-00133543.

[15] Mitchell Kusy and Elizabeth Holloway, Toxic Workplace!: Managing Toxic Personalities and Their Systems of Power (San Francisco: Jossey-Bass, 2009).

13. THE CASE FOR DIVERSITY, EQUITY, INCLUSION, AND BELONGING

[1] "How George Floyd Died, and What Happened Next," New York Times, July 29, 2022, www.nytimes.com/article/george-floyd.html.

[2] George Anders, "Who's Vaulting into the C-Suite? Trends Changed Fast in 2022," LinkedIn, February 1, 2023, www.linkedin.com/pulse/whos-vaulting-c-suite-trends-changed-fast-2022-george-anders.

[3] Kenneth Pucker, "Companies Are Scaling Back Sustainability Pledges. Here's What They Should Do Instead," Harvard Business Review, August 20, 2024, https://hbr.org/2024/08/companies-are-scaling-back-sustainability-pledges-heres-what-they-should-do-instead.

[4] "The 2022 Corporate Racial Equity Tracker," JUST Capital, May 30, 2022, https://justcapital.com/reports/2022-corporate-racial-equity-tracker.

5 "The 2022 Corporate Racial Equity Tracker."
6 Dedrick Asante-Muhammed et al., "An Initial Overview of Racial Economic Equity Commitments," National Community Reinvestment Coalition, February 13, 2024, https://ncrc.org/an-initial-overview-of-racial-economic-equity-commitments-by-banks.
7 Shaun Harper, "Where Is the $200 Billion Companies Promised After George Floyd's Murder?," Forbes, October 17, 2022, www.forbes.com/sites/shaunharper/2022/10/17/where-is-the-200-billion-companies-promised-after-george-floyds-murder.
8 Jaclyn Diaz, "Florida Gov. Ron DeSantis Signs a Bill Banning DEI Initiatives in Public Colleges," NPR, May 15, 2023, www.npr.org/2023/05/15/1176210007/florida-ron-desantis-dei-ban-diversity.
9 Harper, "Where Is the $200 Billion?"
10 John A. Powell, Stephen Menendian, and Wendy Ake, "Targeted Universalism," Othering & Belonging Institute at UC Berkeley, May 2019, https://belonging.berkeley.edu/targeted-universalism.
11 Erica Volini et al., "2020 Global Human Capital Trends Report," Deloitte Insights, Deloitte Development LLC, 2020, https://www2.deloitte.com/cn/en/pages/human-capital/articles/global-human-capital-trends-2020.html.
12 Joan C. Williams and Jamie Dolkas, "Data-Driven Diversity," Harvard Business Review, March–April 2022, https://hbr.org/2022/03/data-driven-diversity.
13 Williams and Dolkas, "Data-Driven Diversity."
14 Adapted from Melissa J. Nixon, "A Prayer for Women Leaders," LinkedIn, March 8, 2019, www.linkedin.com/pulse/prayer-women-leaders-melissa-j-nixon.

14. COACHING UP, POWER DYNAMICS, AND CHANGE MANAGEMENT

1 "Kübler-Ross Change Curve," Elisabeth Kübler-Ross (website), accessed August 5, 2024, www.ekrfoundation.org/5-stages-of-grief/change-curve.
2 Andrew Bauld, "Changing for the Better," Harvard Graduate School of Education, accessed September 7, 2024, www.gse.harvard.edu/hgse100/story/changing-better.
3 Bauld, "Changing for the Better."